SO YOU WANT TO BE A TEACHER?

A guide for current and prospective students in Australia

Phil Ridden and Tracey Gray

First published 2013
by ACER Press, an imprint of
Australian Council *for* Educational Research Ltd,
Camberwell, Victoria, Australia

This edition published 2020
by Edwest Publishing,
Joondalup, Western Australia
www.edwestpublishing.biz

ISBN: 978-0-9925481-3-1

CONTENTS

FOREWORD

A teacher's job is one of the most vital in our community. Teachers not only teach our students subjects such as maths, science and English, they also develop our children to go on to become the next generation of leaders and professionals to run our country.

As you will learn in the pages of this book, a teacher's role is varied and challenging, but mostly it is rewarding. Teachers are in a unique position to make a difference to the future of our children, and also to our communities.

In a global and competitive world, quality education and quality teaching has become more important than ever. We have many quality teachers in Australia, but to ensure our future prosperity, we need to keep encouraging young passionate minds to enter the teaching profession to ensure our children get quality education outcomes and the best start in life.

Teachers not only develop their students academically, but they develop their students in a personal sense as well. Teachers play an important role in guiding and developing students to be all they can be.

So *you want* to be *a teacher?* provides vital information about the road to becoming a teacher, including what makes a good teacher, what to expect from university life and how to prepare for a teaching career. In the course of this book you will meet many inspiring teachers, each of whom are finalists in the National Excellence in Teaching Awards (NEiTA). These awards recognise teachers for their outstanding work.

This year 's finalists included teachers who created state-of-the-art JCT learning areas, taught in classrooms where 35 per cent of the children did not have English as their first language and used innovative techniques to improve student outcomes.

As Chairman of the NEiTA Foundation and the Australian Scholarships Group (ASG) — a dedicated supporter of the awards since they commenced in 1994 — I have met many wonderful teachers and it is always inspiring meeting the NEiTA finalists.

We need to keep supporting teachers by recognising the great work they do, and encouraging and supporting those who want to enter the profession.

So *you want* to *be a teacher?* is a great resource in helping you to work out whether the teaching profession is the right fit for you — by informing you of the training involved, the realities of being a teacher, and the current issues impacting the teaching profession.

Reading this book will help you to make an informed choice so that if you decide to enter the profession it will be with dedication and passion.

Terry O'Connell, NEiTA Chairman

ACKNOWLEDGEMENTS

Despite the authors' own experience as teachers, we wanted to include in this book the voices of other teachers. The Australian Scholarships Group generously assisted us with this, by allowing us to connect with finalists in the National Excellence in Teaching Awards. We thank ASG for their support. Of the finalists we contacted, at a busy time of the year, around 150 provided responses to our questions. We are grateful to them for their willingness to share their insights. We believe the reader will be grateful too, because each comment comes from a successful, well grounded teacher who is passionate about their work. They ensure that this book is not simply a theoretical treatise on teaching. We regret that we were not able to use all the comments we received, but we thank all those who participated. We have selected the comments which seemed most helpful, without trying to be pedantic about a balance between early childhood, primary and secondary teachers, nor between government and non-government schools.

We also thank Ruby Dawes — who may become a teacher — for the useful feedback which she provided; and Kate Hewett for permission to use the material in 'Starting out'.

ABOUT THE AUTHORS

Dr Phil Ridden has a broad field of experience and a strong passion for teaching and learning, and for growing school leaders. Both of these were developed over many years as a primary and secondary teacher, curriculum writer and consultant, professional learning consultant, deputy principal and principal, school board member and parent in government and independent schools, as well as through his work as a consultant, speaker and writer.

Dr Ridden is the author of a number of books on teaching and school leadership, including *For those who teach, Keys to school leadership* (co-authored with John De Nobile), and *What teachers need* to *know about assessment and reporting* (co-authored with Sandy Heldsinger). See https://www.philridden.biz

Tracey Gray is Principal of Sapphire Coast Anglican College in NSW. She has a desire to make a difference to children, teachers and both aspiring and current school leaders, developed over years in training and development in private enterprise, managing many educational initiatives for systems and sectors, and in school teaching and leadership. Her passion is to ensure that education is a positive experience for all and that all students achieve their full potential.

INTRODUCTION

So you want to be a teacher ... or are at least considering the possibility?

The purpose of this book is to assist you to better understand what the teaching profession involves. It is written by two people who are passionate about teaching. Throughout the book you will hear from many successful practising teachers, all of whom were finalists in the National Excellence in Teaching Awards. (Each quote includes the school level and sector in which the teacher was working at the time.) Woven through their words and practical advice, you will hear their passion for teaching, too.

But teaching is not for everyone. So this book attempts to describe the realities of teaching — the frustrations, stresses, myths — because we want you to have a realistic and honest assessment of the pathway to teaching and the experience of teaching. If you choose teaching for a career, choose it with your heart *and* your head.

Everyone has been to school, but a student only sees a small section of what a teacher does. So we begin by explaining the role of a teacher, to show what teachers actually do.

We then explore why you might want to be a teacher and the qualities of a successful teacher, so that you can consider whether you fit the profile. Then we balance this by discussing why you might not want to be a teacher, not to discourage you, but to ensure you know the full story, not just the warm and fluffy part

You'll want to know about the pay and conditions, but may feel awkward about asking, so we discuss this too.

Then we look at how you will train to be teacher – the university course and related work. This connects with choices about where you might specialise or focus your career, because this may influence your choice of university units as well as your employment decisions.

If you become a teacher, it is helpful to know what employers will expect of you and how you can ensure you succeed, so we discuss this, with the help of advice from those in the field.

Because education is changing, just like any other industry, and it will typically be four years before you are ready to begin teaching, we offer a peek into the future.

We then hear from a teacher who reflects on her first year in the profession. The final section outlines one teacher's journey. It highlights the different experiences students may have of education and the different motivations that drive people to become teachers. If you are considering teaching, you probably found school reasonably successful and enjoyable. This story, on the other hand, provides a real-life account of the distress that school can cause for some students, but has a surprising ending, because the distressed student became a teacher.

We hope you find this book helpful as you consider teaching.

We add a disclaimer. Teacher salaries which are quoted in this book, and courses offered by Australian tertiary institutions which are detailed in the Appendix, change from year to year, as may pathways to teaching and government regulations affecting teachers. You should check for up-to-date information about such matters.

1

WHY WOULD I WANT TO BE A TEACHER?

> *I wanted to help people be able to see the world in different ways and felt that the education of young people was the best way to do this. This motivation still keeps me going; it is absolutely possible to change the lens through which people see, and it is incredibly rewarding to see students make really positive change in their lives. (Jeff Thomas, secondary, Catholic)*

We begin by explaining the role of a teacher, to show what teachers actually do with their time. We then consider why you might want to be a teacher. We do this by considering what attracts people to teaching and what keeps them there or motivates them.

What do teachers do?

There is more to teaching than standing in front of a class and lecturing or issuing instructions. Teaching is a complex process. An influential meta-analysis of research identified five major dimensions of excellent teaching:

- identifying essential representations of a subject — expert teachers have deep content knowledge, can integrate prior knowledge with new information, can identify the most significant content within their broader knowledge as relevant to a given class or teaching situation, and can problem-solve, think on their feet and respond deeply to student queries within their subject area
- guiding learning through classroom interactions — expert teachers have deep understanding of multidimensional, complex, context- specific classroom environments and can create optimal learning climates to suit different situations
- monitoring learning and providing feedback — expert teachers are adept at assessing and tracking student performance and progress, understanding why students are achieving or struggling, and providing constructive feedback to improve student learning
- attending to affective attributes — expert teachers have respect for students and passion for teaching and learning
- influencing student outcomes — expert teachers engage students, enhance students' surface and deep learning, develop their self-efficacy, provide them with appropriate

challenges and goals, and generally have a positive influence on their achievement. [1]

Clearly, teaching is not the simple task it may appear to the student. Teachers' work is complex; it requires knowledge of a lot more than the lesson content. Within the classroom, teachers do a great deal more than simply convey information. Because students differ in their pre-existing knowledge, abilities and preferred learning styles, teachers are constantly thinking about how students are responding, which students are struggling and which need further challenges, how to deal with students who are disrupting the learning of others, how to engage students better, how to help students to learn better, and so on.

A teacher's day also consists of work outside the classroom. Teachers are given time for duties other than teaching or non-contact time to attend to some of this work, although they will usually take time beyond the school day.

In a recent Australian survey, full-time teachers reported that they spent, on average, around 40 to 50 per cent of their working time on face-to-face teaching. The rest of the time is spent on other activities, such as lesson preparation, supervision of students outside of school hours, mentoring of colleagues, meetings and professional learning.[2]

Depending on a teacher's particular teaching role, the non-contact tasks may include preparing lessons and teaching materials; setting up and cleaning up materials and equipment; marking student work; supervising students during recess and lunch breaks and before and after school; talking with students (supporting them in their work or their lives); locating and selecting resources; meeting with parents; tidying the classroom; collaborating with colleagues on a wide range of issues related to teaching, student wellbeing or school life; supporting or mentoring colleagues; organising special school and classroom events such as excursions, camps, concerts , assemblies, carnivals and open days; communicating with parents, in written newsletters, meetings, and individual interviews; participating in school decision-making processes; supervising co-curricular activities; reporting student progress to parents, school leaders and government authorities; managing the work of learning assistants, technicians and other support staff; liaising with colleagues, including other teachers and counsellors; liaising with external consultants, such as therapists, doctors and psychologists; participating in professional learning experiences; and supervising pre-service teaching practicums. The list is by no means exhaustive.

While some of these tasks may seem intimidating at this stage, the purpose of a four-year pre-service degree is to equip you to do them. The exciting part of what teachers do is that it is always changing, always diverse and no two days are the same.

> *I work individually and in small groups with students, I plan ahead for their learning and abilities in order to support and challenge each and every one of the diverse learners in my classroom. I am a nurse, a therapist, a caring ear to listen to the troubles of my students. I help*

them sort through friendship problems and family troubles. I run a chess club and a science club during and after school. I meet with parents about their children. I also enjoy strong friendships with my colleagues and we share the journey of teaching together. (Caitlin O'Keeffe, primary, Catholic)

Being in front of the class is only a very small, but important, part of my day. I can also be found sharing ideas with colleagues, counselling students, helping students understand a concept that they didn't get in class, solving computer issues, searching for visual stimuli from the web to enhance my classes, performing administrivia, contacting parents, setting assessment tasks, photocopying, writing merit awards, marking, marking, marking — the list is endless! (Roslyn Penson, secondary, government)

Plan lessons, review lessons, call parents, catch up with students in crises, finish off marking work, purchase new and replace old equipment, email other media teachers for ideas, network, plan the next year's social event, meet with the student council leaders, act on a parent query, meet with the line manager, undertake professional research or reading, yard duty, prepare displays, and pray that the next class runs smoothly and that all the students in our care are doing well. (Bernard Hart, secondary, independent)

What attracts people to teaching?

What attracted those who are currently teaching? For some it was the apparently generous work conditions – reasonable pay, short days, long holidays. When you are young or a parent needing to provide care for your children outside of school hours, this sounds very appealing. However, most teachers entered teaching in order to make a difference to young lives. Throughout this book, this is a recurring theme. Through the words of exemplary teachers, you will hear words and phrases like passion, commitment, making a difference, helping students, love and inspiration.

The authors have no desire to be unduly warm and mushy, nor to conjure false emotion. However, the reality is that most teachers see teaching as more than a job, more than simply performing a set of tasks. To most teachers teaching is a calling, a vocation and an opportunity to enter the lives of children and youth and to enhance their lives. This is not about making the teacher feel noble and good, but about improving the lives of others.

> *Being able to help a child communicate their needs and interests, understand their goals, motivations, strengths and challenges and then support them to achieve amazing things and show them how they have grown and developed, celebrating their achievements along the way, is really a wonderful ingredient to improve and develop each child's self-esteem and self-belief. In addition, you*

> *get to sing, create, design, invent, explore, imagine, play and have lots of fun each and every day — what more could you want? (Louise Stallard, kindergarten, independent community kindergarten)*

> *[I was attracted to teaching by] my love of people and wanting to use my creativity and sense of justice to improve the lives of the poor and marginalised. I have a background in special education and have had. and valued, the opportunity to teach students who are marginalised in some way, or in implementing programs to improve their lives and give them a voice. (Lynne Moten, Reception to Year 12, independent)*

What attracts you to teaching? Is it an interest which is likely to fade quickly or is it an interest which is grounded in who you are and what you want to do with your life?

Of course, what attracts us at the age of 18 is not what attracts us at age 40. Because of this, and because our life's circumstances, opportunities and needs change over time, some teachers enter and others leave teaching at later stages in their lives. However, among those teachers who appear to be most successful, there is clear evidence that pay, holidays and other material benefits are secondary to a passion to teach, generated by their core values.

What keeps people in teaching?

That which attracts us is not necessarily that which holds us. This is as true about a career as it is about a relationship. In teaching, it is evident in the large number of teachers who leave the profession in the first five years — variously estimated at 25 per cent to 40 per cent.[3] What holds skilled teachers in the profession?

Teachers stay as teachers because of stimulation, challenges, rewards and relationships. It is interesting that many principals and school leaders say that they love their leadership role, but miss the classroom interaction they had with students.

Any job is, to a large degree, the same day by day and week by week. In many ways that is true of teaching. Yet teachers comment that they find the job constantly stimulating and every day and every year different. There are several reasons:

- Although the content of the curriculum may be similar from year to year, the students are different — their interests, their learning styles, their abilities, their personalities and their needs. Therefore, the teaching and relationships are different, so each year is different. This is why some teachers stay in the classroom for 40 years or more.
- Teachers must constantly refine their craft. The essence of teaching is not in delivering instruction, but in facilitating learning. Knowledge of the neuroscience of learning is constantly evolving, and teachers need to understand this to best facilitate learning. The curriculum, also, may be constantly changing, as new knowledge impacts on each

subject area. The use of technology to assist learning is also a constantly evolving field. Teachers must know how they can teach better and engage students more effectively, and stay up to date with new advances in technology and the science of learning. Teachers are lifelong learners.

- The teacher's work is not done when they have presented the lesson, but when the student has understood and integrated the learning. In this regard, each student presents a unique challenge.
- Because teachers are committed to the growth of students, not just intellectually, but also emotionally, socially, spiritually and in all other ways, the relationship with each student, and the support needed for each, is unique.

> *Teaching is never the same — there are new groups of students, there are new developments in the language itself, there are new ways of presenting the curriculum. The advent of technology has opened limitless possibilities for language teachers. (Judy Taylor, secondary, independent)*

> *[What keeps me in teaching is] the ability to continue learning not just about different subject material, but equally as fascinating, about how we learn and what is a quality learning environment. (Mike Jaremczuk, secondary government)*

Most teachers have a strong sense of moral purpose; that is, they want to make a positive difference in the lives of children and youth. Teachers are motivated by seeing the eyes of a struggling student light up with understanding; by their relationship with their students — the shared experiences of joy, sadness, laughter, disappointment, teamwork, friendship and discovery together; by student achievement, success and enjoyment; by seeing their students go on to study further in the field; and by watching small children become independent and confident or adolescents grow into young men and women.

Each of us, from time to time, appreciates some gesture of affirmation — a gift, a word of praise or appreciation, a pay bonus. Teachers spend much of their time alone with students, so parents, colleagues, school leaders and others who might commend them for their work are not there to observe it. They do not receive bonus nor overtime payments, nor time in lieu for extra work. Teachers depend on intrinsic motivation; that is, intangible rewards — indication of progress in a student's learning, a student's growing maturity or change of attitude, hearing a student take pride in something they have learned.

> *Everyday something you could do could change a child's life. You have the potential to make a difference in their lives, and there are only a handful of professions where you get this opportunity. Each day has a reward. (Casey Mills, primary, government)*

> *I love the light bulb moments you see in children. I also love it when you see dramatic change in a child's work. I enjoy the creativity of teaching and that every day is different. (Mark Nelson, primary, Catholic)*

There are some opportunities for teachers to remain in the classroom and take on other responsibilities, thereby gaining recognition for being an exemplary teacher without relinquishing their teaching to become a principal or other leader. These opportunities might include supervising practicums for pre-service teachers, leading curriculum implementation and innovation, designing professional learning for teaching staff, coordinating resources and organising camps and other events. The Australian Professional Standards for Teachers (see Chapter 9) provide the level of 'lead' teacher for teachers who wish to stay in the classroom but take on other responsibilities within the school.

Other rewards

Most people seek from their work:

- A sense of worth, a feeling that our work matters. Teaching matters; it is worth doing; it makes a difference to students' lives. At the risk of being simplistic, adults who did not succeed in schooling are over-represented in prisons and under-represented in employment. In most societies, high quality education is highly valued.
- A sense of achievement, a feeling that we are actually succeeding. While test scores or other measures of academic achievement matter, teachers are also concerned at how students grow in social and emotional ways. There are

many variables involved, and many of these are beyond a teacher's control, but there are many opportunities for teachers to see that they are succeeding in their work, that they are making a difference.

- A sense of community, a feeling that we connect or belong, that we share a common purpose in our work and are supported by others. Schools are communities, in which the older guide and support the youth, and the youth energise the older.[4]

So teaching offers all of these things. Teaching is eminently worthwhile, because it shapes the lives of children and youth. The success and growth of a student provides teachers with a wonderful sense of achievement. Being closely involved in the lives of students and their families, getting to know them well and allowing them to get to know you, celebrating and grieving with colleagues as you support a student — these things create a strong sense of belonging.

2

WOULD I MAKE A GOOD TEACHER?

Do you:

- *love learning?*
- *enjoy innovation?*
- *know you have the ideas to help bring learning alive?*
- *know that sharing your day with young minds is not only a benefit to them but an inspiration to you too?*
- *want an exciting, satisfying, challenging and inspirational lifelong career?*

… then you know you are suited to teaching! (Jennifer Saunders, secondary, Catholic)

Whether you would make a good teacher depends on your personal qualities. In this section we will explore the qualities which are typical of successful teachers, so you can reflect on whether these match your qualities.

What is a good teacher?

Some people assume that if you know something, you can teach it to others. This is not so. Most of us have encountered people who always seem to want to lecture us or teach us things, but from whom we have little interest in learning. Having knowledge does not necessarily make a person an effective teacher. Teaching is an art and a skill.

Many people believe themselves to be experts on teaching because they have been to school. While this is naive given the years of training required to become a teacher, we do all have some insights. You will recall teachers who were or were not effective and influential in your schooling. It may be helpful to think about the 'best' and 'worst' teachers in your school experience and to consider their characteristics, manner and way of teaching. What are the qualities you identify as those needed by teachers?

There is a substantial body of research that contributes to our understanding. The Grattan Institute released a report in 2011 highlighting what makes a good teacher. Key aspects including connection with students, planning, learning intention, lesson sequencing, engagement, questioning technique, metacognition and reflection by students are described as vital in promoting growth in student outcomes.[5]

Many university schools of education list teacher qualities on their websites. For example, La Trobe University suggests that a good teacher should be:

- committed —demonstrates commitment to students and the profession
- communicative — encourages effective two-way communication
- compassionate — caring, empathetic and able to respond to people
- creative — versatile, innovative and open to new ideas
- dependable — honest and authentic in working with others
- flexible — willing to alter plans and directions to assist people in moving toward their goals
- individually perceptive — sees each student as a unique and valuable individual
- knowledgeable — is in a constant quest for knowledge
- motivational — enthusiastic with standards and expectations for students and self
- organised — makes efficient use of time
- patient — is deliberate in coming to conclusions
- personable — establishes and maintains positive mutual working relationships
- positive — thinks positively and enthusiastically about people and what they are capable of becoming

- humorous – knows how to take the tension out of tight situations
- value-based – focuses upon the worth and dignity of human beings.[6]

You will find similar information on the websites of some education systems. The Queensland education department lists these skills and qualities:

- being good at explaining things
- being a people person and enjoying working with a wide range of people
- enthusiasm
- having a strong knowledge in particular subject areas
- being a good time manager
- being able to work in a team as well as using your own initiative
- keeping your cool under pressure
- having patience and a good sense of humour
- being fair-minded
- coping well with change
- enjoying a challenge.[7]

Exemplary teachers add their own emphases. Interestingly, these tend to be less about knowledge of content and more about personal and intellectual qualities.

> *[Teachers need] a capacity to engage students and challenge them at all times with an awareness of their state of mind. ... A capacity to compel students to learn and do their best. A sharp intellect and strong academic background allied with an ability to communicate your knowledge in a clear and effective way. A commitment to differentiating the curriculum based on student ability. A passion for your subject matter and teaching. A capacity to support students with their learning. (Anna Vaxalis, secondary, government)*

> *Today teachers need to be willing to try to create different activities. They need to be logical thinkers as well as being creative. They must be compassionate, empathetic and insightful. (Lynn Thorp. primary, government)*

> *Teachers need to be patient, understanding and fair. They need to have a sense of humour and a willingness to be inventive in order to inspire all children in their classes. (Helen Powell, primary, government)*

> *[Teachers need:]*
>
> - *passion — for what they teach and for the students they are teaching*
> - *patience — which allows students to make mistakes, to develop*
> - *self-control — have the ability to control your reactions and responses*

- *humility — apologise when you are in the wrong*
- *organisation — classrooms need order and planning as a structural foundation*
- *flexibility — be able to respond to situations and students as individuals*
- *the ability to be firm must be able to lead strongly with clear boundaries and expectations. (Steven Reid, middle/secondary, government)*

However, you may find more compelling the opinions of students, such as those recorded by the United Nations Educational, Scientific and Cultural Organisation. Some of these children wrote:

> *The teacher is to the students what the rain is to the field. (Zaira Alexandra Rodriguez Guijarro, 11, Mexico)*
>
> *A good teacher should treat all pupils like his own children. He should answer all questions, even if they are stupid. (Fatoumata, 11, Chad)*
>
> *To become a good teacher, you not only teach the children but you also have to learn from them. (Tasha-Leigh, 12, Jamaica)*
>
> *A good teacher answers the needs of the pupils and not only the needs of the chosen programme. (Omar, 12, Morocco)*
>
> *I like a teacher who helps me think and get answers for myself. (Bongani Sicelo, 9, Zimbabwe)*[8]

It is apparent that in assessing whether you have the qualities to be a teacher, you need to consider not just intellectual capacity, but also personal and relational qualities.

Succeeding in the long term

We indicated earlier that many teachers leave teaching in their early years. For many, the experience of teaching does not match the promise. However, what is important to note here is that the problem may not simply lie with a job that doesn't prove to be exactly what we expected. What also matters is whether we have the personal qualities to cope with the reality.

A group of Australian researchers suggests that teachers who cope with the stresses and frustrations of teaching most effectively are those who are resilient. In their research with beginning and early career teachers, the researchers identified four dimensions of resilience:

- a profession-related dimension enables the teacher to reflect on their work and make changes
- an emotional dimension enables the teacher to deal with feelings of inadequacy
- a social dimension enables the teacher to be comfortable in asking for help
- a motivational dimension enables the teacher to persevere

through difficulties.[9]

These are supported by multiple dimensions of resilience, such as time management and organisational skills, a sense of humour, a positive attitude and the ability to maintain a balance between work and leisure. The authors argue that these various dimensions of resilience can be developed and are drawn on in difficult times. The relevance of this is that, no matter how strong your intellectual and relational skills and your passion to teach, in order to survive as a teacher, you will need resilience. Although resilience can be developed over time with training and experience, you may find it useful to consider whether you are, at heart, a resilient person.

> *I think teachers need to be resilient, they need to have a sense of humour, to be able to adjust to change, fantastic as time managers, to enjoy the company of the young men and women they teach. They need to want to make a difference and believe that they can! They need to be good listeners, be able to take criticism, to back down when they make a mistake — laugh at it, admit it and move on. They need to inspire students to want to do better and also themselves to want to constantly do better. They need to reflect on what worked, what didn't work and be able to change the lesson next time. Teachers need to be flexible and willing to accept change, to read widely and to network with other teachers (Ursula Witham-Young, Year 5 to 12 boys' school, Catholic)*

What if I have a disability?

A disability need not prevent someone from becoming a teacher. While a disability may enable a teacher to better empathise with and assist disabled students, a teacher with a disability is not constrained to teaching students with disabilities. Here are comments from a teacher who is deaf:

> *You can do it. Stay positive. If you enjoy working with children and feel you have lots to offer, then mode! When you study or go to lectures with hearing students, they can learn more about deafness in practical or face-to-face situations, rather than just in theory. It can be hard at times, but you have to persevere to stay positive and the rewards are at the end of the tunnel! (Kathryn Smitt, early childhood, government)*

How can I know if this would suit me?

Whether teaching will suit you will depend on your attitudes to work and to students. Consider answers to these:

- What do you like doing? Teachers enjoy learning and being with people — listening to them, relating to them (not just telling them what they don't know!).
- What do you believe about children and youth? Teachers enjoy being with the young and have confidence in the ability of the next generation to find its way.

- How do you feel about students who struggle to learn? You will encounter plenty of these. Teachers understand that no student hopes to fail. Helping students takes patience, persistence, empathy and targeted assistance. Some people enter teaching because they struggled with some aspect of their own learning. You must be able to empathise with students who don't find school easy — which is not always related to intelligence — and to show that you want to help those students.
- How do you feel about students who are disruptive? Teachers understand that when students are intentionally disruptive and difficult, they need clear boundaries and consequences, but in an environment of care and concern. No student seeks trouble unless their needs are not being met.
- How do you feel about learning? Some students are glad to leave school and look forward to the end of their studies. Teachers love learning, seek knowledge and anticipate being lifelong learners.
- How do you feel about parents and parenting7 It is easy to assume that each student with a 'bad attitude' is the product of parents who have taught him or her that attitude. Experience will show that most parents want the best for their child and are doing the very best they can for their child in the circumstances life has dealt them and with the life experiences they have. Many parents are

embarrassed about their child's inadequacies at school and many are intimidated by teachers whom they see as knowledgeable and judgemental. Successful teachers understand these things and seek to work with parents in a respectful partnership.

- What do you want from a career? Teaching does not fit into a nine to five workday and there are neither overtime payments nor bonuses. Teachers need to please their employer, students and students' parents. Complaints are not handled by the enquiries desk or customer relations department, but by the teachers themselves. Teachers work, much of the time, isolated from other adults. For much of their work, they are their own boss.

To assist you in answering these questions, you might ask family or close friends or the teachers at school who knew you best. Formally, there are a number of surveys and quizzes that you can do online that will suggest the types of careers you may be suited to. You might also visit a university and talk to academic staff in the school of education. They have been classroom teachers and can discuss with you what being a teacher is like, what teaching practicums involve and what the course entails. Visiting your local school and volunteering will give you an up-close perspective of schools and what a day in school is like. Look within and think hard about who you are, what you can offer to children and youth and what you like to do.

The authors know of no formal interview process to determine a person's suitability for teaching, neither at university entrance nor at the time of registration as a qualified teacher. Therefore, there is currently no effective external judgement of a person's suitability. It is not until a teacher seeks employment that an interviewer makes a personal judgement about the person's suitability for teaching and for the culture of that school. It is possible that this may change in the future as the Commonwealth Government is proposing:

> a new national approach for admission into teaching courses that recognises the personal qualities needed for teaching in addition to academic achievement. This will help make sure only people who have the passion and attributes needed for teaching enter these courses. This could include:
>
> - interviews to ensure students have the emotional intelligence, resilience and commitment to teaching
> - a portfolio of activities like sport coaching or community involvement, to demonstrate values and aptitude
> - a written statement outlining why the applicant wants to be a teacher.[10]

However, others want to raise the academic standards of entrants into teaching courses. At the time of writing, the media reported an 'unprecedented stoush between the NSW and federal governments and the university sector over teacher entry requirements'.[11] Universities have expressed support for the Commonwealth Government's proposal to assess the personal aptitude of entrants to teaching courses, but may not support the NSW government plan to raise academic entrance requirements. Under the NSW government plan, students would need to achieve a band 5, or 80 per cent, in at least three senior secondary school subjects, including English, to qualify for entry to university teaching courses.

Attempts to regulate entry standards and qualities of entrants into pre-service teaching courses will not be easy to agree upon nor to implement. However, such standards are important: Teaching is complex. Although many people can instruct, not everyone can teach. So, intellectual ability matters. Students and parents are very cynical about teachers who presume to correct student work when their own work is littered with errors. So, academic standards matter. Parents hand their impressionable children into the care of teachers whom they cannot choose, but who have significant influence on the lives of children. So, values and character matter.

A key part of every teacher education degree is time spent in classrooms, usually on a number of occasions, beginning with a short stint consisting primarily of observation and culminating in an extended final practicum when the trainee is required to do extensive teaching. These practicums are an excellent opportunity to decide whether you are suited to teaching, through exposure to both the craft of teaching and the demands of teaching. The practicums also enable you to assess the age groups to which you feel most suited. Many teachers refine their opinions about the age of students they most prefer teaching after their classroom experiences.

> *The most important thing for a trainee is to examine the reasons or motivations they have for entering teaching. If they have chosen teaching because they couldn't get into medicine or engineering or because the hours of work and holidays seemed appealing, I would urge them to find an alternative career If they have chosen teaching because they wanted to make a difference to the lives of children and contribute to the most important profession within any society, then they are likely to be very well prepared for their first teaching job. (Kim Doust, principal, primary, government)*

3

THE REALITIES OF TEACHING

So many children — such diverse needs; so little support — so few resources! (Catherine Pike, early childhood, government)

Within the last 10 years, frustration and difficulties have come about in trying to meet all stakeholders' requests or requirements, rather than focusing on the individual needs of the learner. (Yvonne Rinaldi, principal, primary, independent)

In teaching, as in any job, there are frustrations. In this section, we identify these, which also helps to explain why some teachers leave teaching. This section may seem a little 'negative', but our intention is to ensure that you make a decision based on an understanding of the issues teachers face.

So, what are the particular frustrations and difficulties faced by teachers?

An overcrowded curriculum

The Australian Curriculum considers the 'core' subjects of education from foundation through to Year 10 to be English, mathematics, science, history, geography, languages other than English, the arts, technologies, health and physical education, and civics and citizenship.

Some educators have raised concerns that, even within these core subjects, the curriculum contains more content than can be taught in depth within the given timeframes.[12] Another concern raised is that a focus on student and school performance in the National Assessment Program — Literacy and Numeracy (NAPLAN) minimises the time available for other subject areas.[13]

Increasingly, schools also address additional skills and social issues as part of the formal curriculum or through add-on programs. This may include education around obesity and nutrition, kitchen gardening, smoking, drugs and alcohol, first aid, sex education, sustainability and environmental design, ethics and values, community service, financial literacy, intercultural understanding, critical and creative thinking, specific sports or music programs and so on.

There is a strong view in our society that whatever problems occur in the community, schools are to blame for causing them, through inappropriate curriculum or poor teaching, or should be responsible for correcting them, through additions and reforms to an already crowded curriculum.

Youth unemployment, crime, mental and physical health issues, bullying and violence, drug and alcohol abuse, even discourtesy are all seen by some to be the responsibility of schools. Schools have long borne the responsibilities of the community. Schools are a microcosm of society; society's issues are all reflected in the school.

> *[Frustrations include the] crowded curriculum — always feeling that you haven't quite done everything in every subject area. There needs to be greater respect by the general public —not always adding shortcomings in society (lack of manners, smoking, drugs, lack of students being able to swim and so on) to the curriculum. (Nan van Dissel, primary, government)*

Administrative demands

Teachers have numerous responsibilities beyond their classroom interaction with students. Teachers are required to plan and prepare lessons, source resources and materials, do photocopying and filing, take notes at meetings, handle student permission and absence forms and monies for activities and equipment and so on. Within the first three years of teaching, graduate or provisional teachers are expected to complete an application process to obtain status as a registered teacher. This process may involve keeping a folio of work, obtaining references from colleagues and mentors, and writing statements and providing evidence to show the graduate has addressed certain criteria and met the professional standards required to become a registered teacher. Once registered, teachers are required to undertake and keep a record of their professional learning in order to maintain their registration.

A significant amount of teachers' time is invested in assessment and reporting. Teachers are required to assess and report on students' performance at a number of levels. This involves extensive setting and marking of students' classroom tasks and homework; providing detailed constructive feedback to students on their performance, progress and behaviour; reporting formally and informally to parents; liaising with school leaders regarding student performance at the level of individual students, classes, year levels, whole-school and state and national benchmarks; and complying with state and national assessment and reporting mandates.

Teachers are required to carry out summative and formative assessment. Summative assessment includes tests that give a quantitative grade, rank or score, usually for the purposes of comparing students' performance. Formative assessment is often more detailed and intensive qualitative assessment designed to reveal what students know and can do, and to diagnose areas of student weakness, such as topics that a class or individual students have not understood or tasks they are unable to successfully complete. Formative assessment should result in constructive feedback to help students to learn, as well as information that allows teachers to modify their teaching strategies, revisit content or tailor individualised programs to improve teaching and learning.

Governments and systems have increased accountability demands. Testing of students and assessment of teachers have placed teachers under pressure to perform, even though they have no control over the 'raw material' they work with, and even though there is a plethora of other factors beyond teachers' control which also affect the performance of students. Politicians simply reflect the views of the local or wider community, and the community is constantly demanding that teachers 'fix' the problems of children and youth.

> *The administration, the politics and the endless demands placed on classroom teachers are what I find to be the most difficult and frustrating. (Laura Bond, primary, government)*

> *Teachers leave because there are too many walls and obstacles, too much 'extra stuff' that takes away from real and meaningful connections with children, too many 'we've always done it this way' attitudes, and too little recognition for what they do. Teachers who teach with heart will put up with the knocks and stay because they believe in what they do ... but sadly many find it just far too tiring and frustrating to keep on getting up again.*

(David Gilkes, early childhood, government)

Balancing and achieving change

Creating change in schools is difficult So is choosing what to change and how to change it Some teachers are frustrated by the frequency of changes to curriculum and expectations; others are frustrated by the difficulty in implementing significant change.

Change is a constant in most workplaces. However, it is wrong to assume that all teachers object to change. Many teachers enjoy the challenge of new ideas and exploring new ways to work — especially if they see a glimmer of possibility that this can support students' learning. Often what teachers seek is a 'voice' in the change process. Many changes are imposed on teachers by schools, and on schools by systems and governments, without clear explanation as to the purpose of the changes and how they will be implemented.

> *All teachers need to embrace change in education at every opportunity, from technology to curriculum to teaching strategies. Education needs to change continually just as society does. (Deborah Tanham, special education, Catholic)*

Myths about teaching

Teachers are sometimes frustrated at the public perception of a teacher's life – good pay, short days, long holidays. There are benefits in these things, but life is not simply as it appears for a teacher! The most common myths are listed below.

Teachers work short days and take long holidays

Unquestionably, this is a perk. Many teachers who are parents find it convenient to be able to care for and enjoy their own children during the vacation. However, as explained in a later section, a teacher's work does not fit into a six-hour day. Many teachers begin at 7.00 a.m. or stay at school until 6.00 p.m., and most take work home. Teachers do not have the same formal holidays as students, and, informally, some holiday time is spent in professional learning courses, preparation and follow-up. As students need a holiday to recharge, so do teachers. You may be surprised to see how tired students – and teachers – get during the school day and the school term.

Teachers think about the job during the day and then let it go

Because teachers are involved in students' lives, they often find it difficult to tum off, to put the students, if not the work, out of their minds. It is interesting that teachers often 'talk shop' at parties and social events. This is partly because many find it difficult to stop thinking about their work and their students.

Teachers have no responsibility

This myth assumes that the teacher does the teaching and, if the student fails to learn, it is the student's fault. In reality, however, teachers have both a moral and a legal responsibility to ensure that each student succeeds as well as they are able, and there are many processes which monitor how well a teacher's students are learning, and, by inference, how well the teacher is teaching. A difficulty for teachers is that they have no control over the students' intellect, family circumstances, social-emotional issues, prior learning and so on. Teachers also have a legal 'duty of care'; that is, they are responsible for the safety and wellbeing of their students. Often teachers will spend many hours outside of the school day consulting and planning to better support a student — talking with colleagues, consultants and parents and devising programs and lessons.

> *Many teachers are so focused on the day-to-day doing the best they can with the children they work alongside that they sometimes find it hard to channel some of their energy into being advocates for both children and the profession in the wider community. It is vital that we do so if we are to bring about change. (David Gilkes, early childhood. government)*

Teaching is easy

This myth goes that teaching young students involves just playing games with them all day, and that teaching older students is simply about setting work and helping students who can't do it. While most teachers enjoy being with their students, they have a responsibility to ensure students learn, whatever age they are. Being a teacher is not the same as being a babysitter, playmate or youth worker.

Teaching is taxing. There will be days you go home physically, mentally and emotionally exhausted. You will have been on your feet all day and given your all, yet go home feeling that you have achieved nothing. Every teacher knows the feeling of referring to material taught the previous day, only to be greeted with blank faces of students who seem to have no recollection of the lesson at all.

There are many beginning teachers who struggle with the life of a school — the unpredictability, the interruptions and disruptions, the social and emotional issues that teachers are constantly confronted with. Of course, good schools try to provide an environment which enables students and teachers to be focused on learning as much as possible, but you cannot control the thinking, attitudes and behaviours of several hundred children or teenagers.

Why do teachers leave teaching?

There are a number of reasons why teachers leave teaching. Some teachers feel that their university experience did not equip them well for the realities of the classroom. While pre-service teachers complete practicums throughout their university programs, these experiences are often only a snippet of teaching, and are so well structured that they do not fully reflect the reality of a teacher's first appointment. Typically practicums are conducted during the middle of a term and may not show how to prepare for the beginning of the year, the end of a term, excursions, communicating with parents, putting on the school assembly, writing reports, dealing with aggressive parents, creating curricula, planning lessons, using assessment to determine planning or finalising the year.

Some graduates leave university assuming that their studies are behind them. New teachers are provided with Provisional Teacher Registration, but must, within three years, gain full registration by achieving the Australian Institute for Teaching and School Leadership (AITSL) Proficient Standard.[14] Ongoing professional learning is essential to retain registration, so teachers who are not committed to lifelong learning may not find the profession suitable and may leave for this reason.

> *Everyone has been to school and so there is a common misconception that teaching is an easy 9 to 3 job with 10 weeks holiday a year. Nothing could be further from the*

> *truth! If you choose teaching as your 'fall back' career on this basis, you will be sadly disappointed. However, if you want to make a difference in the lives of children and truly believe that you have something to offer, then go for it. (Lea Arnold, primary, government)*

> *I find another misconception about teaching kindergarten is that all we do is colour in and draw pictures. I have students in my classroom that are currently achieving end of Year 2 outcomes in mathematics. If they were not given the opportunities to develop these concepts in class then they would not have shown such amazing development. (Liam Clayton, primary/special education, government)*

The point has been made strongly that teaching is demanding. It can be difficult for teachers to tum off, and the intensity of the role can take its toll on a teacher's health. It is important that a teacher has a strong network of family and friends and manages their time efficiently to ensure they find personal time.

A recent report found that teachers lamented a lack of meaningful feedback, with 66 per cent of teachers commenting that feedback and performance appraisals were meaningless.[15] The initial year or years can be daunting, isolating and stressful, and new teachers need to seek feedback that encourages them and provides guidance during this stage.

While schools are busy places, teaching can be quite an isolating occupation. Once children come into the classroom, generally the teacher is alone with them and can feel overwhelmed and unsure of what they are doing. New teachers need to ensure they regularly reflect with a colleague, seek mentors and team-teach from time to time. Sometimes, the school assigns a new teacher a mentor, typically a senior teacher or other successful and experienced colleague; however, some new teachers who left the profession felt that they could not aspire to the level of proficiency of their mentor and this made them feel even more inadequate.

Teaching in rural and remote parts of Australia can be particularly isolating, especially if the school is extremely small and far away from towns and social networks. Having little access to other teachers to support them is difficult in remote contexts. Even in rural schools, there may be no other teacher teaching the same subject or the same year level to offer support and brainstorm ideas. The teacher then feels on their own in developing creative and engaging lessons day after day. It may also mean that problems are not resolved, and so magnify. Many schools are positively addressing teacher isolation through coaching, mentoring, professional learning teams, internet forums and professional development. Digital communication is also a significant aid.

Isolation may be cultural as well as geographical. Teachers may find themselves teaching in communities which hold values different from their own, or in Indigenous communities or ethnic communities, where a lack of understanding of the values and norms of the group may bring teachers into conflict with students and parents.

> *I initially felt overwhelmed and wondered what on earth I was doing, but that quickly changed once I started working with the children. ... Working with families was the hardest part of the job to learn after that there are so many opinions and beliefs. They weren't necessarily mine, but I had to take them into account when I was teaching their child. (Meredith Dick, director, early childhood, government)*

How stressful is teaching?

Every job has some degree of stress, and it is wrong to assume that teaching is unique in this regard. However, managing and teaching a classroom of 30, or perhaps more, children or teenagers can certainly be stressful. There is an urgency about teaching which pushes the teacher on from week to week. Even experienced teachers often end the school year physically, mentally and emotionally exhausted. Teachers' strong sense of moral purpose and the desire to ensure that they offer students the best teaching they can pushes some teachers to work long hours. There will always be some students who struggle despite the teacher's best efforts and this preys on a teacher's desire to see them succeed.

> *Teaching is a noble profession, to which, to be successful, you need to devote much of your time. To achieve a life balance, try to make home life free of school life. I would*

rather stay at school late to complete something than take it home. When I am home I am at home. (Garry Brown, secondary, government)

I try to get all my work finished at school before going home. I think that it is important you have a balanced lifestyle because if you're not careful you could end up spending all your time at school. There is always something you can find to do. (Creed Yorke, primary, Catholic)

I try to make sure that my weekends are mine and not do any schoolwork on Saturday or Sunday and I try not to work after a certain time at night, but I am not always successful. I make sure that my family and friends come first and I spend as much time with them as I can. (Rebecca Armstrong, primary government)

4

PAY AND CONDITIONS

It will not be easy, especially in early years. You will earn the students' respect through hard work, firmness and fairness, and not by being one of their friends. You will have to give up your evenings and weekends many times to achieve the above. Once established, teaching is a joy — most of the time. If you do not enjoy teaching. but do it as a job, for the money, give up! (Tom Stone, senior secondary, independent)

We have made a strong case for teaching as a serving occupation, which people take up for reasons which are closer to their heart than pay and conditions. Nevertheless, it is reasonable to ask about pay and conditions and to ensure you know what you may expect if you become a teacher.

Salary

Teacher salaries vary between states, sectors, systems and schools. Because each state operates its own education system, salaries are state-based for government schools, with Catholic and independent schools setting their own scales. However, there is a close parity between them. While one sector or state may move ahead for a time, others soon match or exceed that standard. In most schools, teachers are paid according to a scale, which provides for an increase each year until around 10 years of experience. While it is possible to negotiate a unique salary, this is only possible in independent schools, and in very few of them. Promotional positions, such as leadership roles, are also typically paid according to a defined scale.

Current salary scales for teachers in government schools can be found on state education system websites. State comparisons for four-year trained teachers as at the time of printing are shown in Table 4.1.

Progress from one step to the next on the scale is annual and usually automatic (assuming satisfactory performance). However, in many systems and schools a teacher who has reached the 'top' of the scale may apply to move to a higher level if they meet specified criteria. (These salaries are constantly being re-negotiated and expectations adjusted, so this table should be seen as a guide only.)

STATE/TERRITORY	SCALE	RANGE
Australian Capital Territory	9 steps	$68,022 to $101,821
New South Wales	9 steps	$68,929 to $102,806
Northern Territory	9 steps	$73,334 to $105,172
Queensland	12 steps	$61,806 to $101,000
South Australia	9 steps	$68,126 to $98,806
Tasmania	10 steps	$64,827 to $97,763
Victoria	11 steps	$67,558 to $101,260
Western Australia	9 steps	$70,137 to $109,089

Table 4.1 Salary scales for teachers in government schools[16]

Hours

Clearly, teachers work when students are at school. The actual hours of a school day vary from school to school, but are usually around six hours per day. In addition, most schools require staff to be at school perhaps 20 or 30 minutes before the school day starts. You may also be required on the premises for staff meetings and other events after school hours. A teacher's day does not start and finish with the bell, and requires some flexibility.

Lesson preparation and follow-up, and a host of other responsibilities described earlier, mostly take place out of school hours.

Working flexible hours

Flexitime is not part of a typical teacher 's work. The reason is obvious — students are required to be at school for particular hours, and those are the core times when a teacher must work. On a 'sluggish' day, a teacher does not have the luxury of asking the students to amuse themselves while the teacher has a coffee, answers some emails, and generally gets himself or herself ready for the day. When the bell rings to start the day, the teacher must be ready to go. Some teachers arrive at school early, so that they can prepare themselves and any resources they need before students arrive.

There is some flexibility in a teacher's use of their non-contact time, although others may organise some of that time for them with parent interviews, meetings with colleagues and other commitments.

Holidays

School vacations amount to around 12 weeks per year. However, there is nothing which guarantees that teachers have all this time to themselves to laze about exotic beaches. The school may require teachers to attend for several days when students are not present, especially at the beginning and end of the school year. To maintain their registration, teachers must participate in professional learning, and increasingly, this is held during vacation time. During vacations, teachers collaborate with colleagues to plan the next term's programs, or to review the success of the previous term and the achievements of students. For none of this are they paid overtime.

> *Our holidays are not just for having time off. There are many things that need to be done: marking of books, evaluation and planning for the next term and year and special programs to cater for the individual needs of the children in our class. (Toni Pullen, primary, government)*

Working alone, working in teams

There are times when a teacher's work is lonely work, when the teacher is the only adult in the classroom. However, this model is changing. Increasingly, teachers are supported in the classroom with learning assistants (also known as teacher assistants or education assistants). A learning assistant is not (usually) a trained teacher, but is employed either to work with individual students with high needs because of disability or to support the teachers with all students. An assistant might work alongside the teacher or with a small group or individual inside or outside the classroom. This makes the teacher a manager of staff, because it is the teacher who is responsible for the learning and who must direct what the assistant does, ensure they know how to do it, monitor that they are doing it correctly and redirect or train them when necessary. The teacher cannot simply hand an assistant a group of students and tell the assistant to teach them.

Increasingly, too, teachers work in teams. While each may have responsibility for a student group on their own, the team may have planned together; the team may include a teacher with expertise teaching students with learning difficulties or may allocate teachers to focus on differing learning areas (subjects) or topics; students may rotate through groups; students may spend some time as a large group (perhaps four or five classes) and then break into smaller groups; learning assistants and volunteer parents may assist; students may cycle out of the classroom to obtain individual support. While there is no single model, there is a desire among teachers to explore other configurations than the traditional model of one teacher and 30 students behind a closed door. The saying 'It takes a whole village to raise a child' also applies to schools: It takes a whole school to educate a student. Teachers need to collaborate with colleagues, support staff and other professionals to ensure the best teaching and learning, and the best environment for growth, is provided for each student.

Job availability

The availability of work varies from time to time, as does the supply of teachers. However, as far as we can anticipate at present, there is a continuing need for teachers. Because there are many 'baby boomer' teachers, predictions suggest that there may be a shortage of teachers in the next decade or so. This is exacerbated by the trend among younger people to change careers regularly, leaving, entering or re-entering teaching during their working lives. There are many teaching roles which are available part-time, although they are well sought after. As with any job, it helps to be as flexible and as available as possible; that is, being willing to teach a range of year levels, a range of subjects in a range of locations, and even across the sectors.

Most schools are happy to employ new graduates. However, it is important to remember that the qualifications and eligibility criteria for teaching are very specific and people do not apply for teaching roles unless they meet these conditions. Therefore, if 20 teachers apply for one job, every one of them can (technically) do the job. Why should an employer choose you?

They may choose you because:

- you have achieved exceptionally high standards in your course work
- you have achieved exceptionally high grades for your teaching practicums, especially the final practicum
- you show that you have a teacher's heart — a passion for learning and for your students
- you show that you will 'fit' the school — that is, you understand and are committed to the values of the school or system you are applying to, and want to be there; it is not just a stop gap until you can get a job in a 'better' school
- you have something additional to offer — skills in sport, music, performance; a proven record as a leader; additional qualifications and so on.

> *When searching for a job, take your resume to schools in your area and ask to personally hand it to the principal. When you get the job, be organised. Have a clear direction before you start the term and front-end assessment tasks so you know where you're headed. (Rebecca Brown, middle school, government)*

> *Have knowledge of content, intelligence and enthusiasm. Have a sense of humour. No 'know-all' attitudes. A willingness to take direction. Someone who likes children! Who sees the 'big picture' of education. Someone who is happy to write — programs, reports,*

grant applications ... (Gayle Cameron. principal, primary. government)

Locations of jobs

There are schools wherever there are people. Teachers keenly seek schools in city locations or popular coastal towns, so many new graduates are obliged to take whatever positions they can get, and these are often in the less popular or remote locations.

There are considerable benefits to teaching outside the cities. Most teachers who have taught in remote settings state that it was the most rewarding and challenging experience of their lives. Remote schools are fascinating, vastly different from each other and exist in all sectors. They are settings where you can learn about the importance of community, where the community is generally supportive of teachers, where teachers connect socially as well as professionally. Many teachers also enjoy the lifestyle of a rural appointment — the slower pace of life and fewer distractions and demands on their time.

I felt very fortunate to have some years of teaching experience under my belt when I went to work in a remote community. Although I was new to the community, I was not new to teaching. Therefore, without the 'first year out' worries of classroom management, planning and assessment weighing me down, I was able to concentrate on learning as much as I could about the history, culture and language of the community in which I was living and working. I feel that foregrounding and valuing their culture and language was one thing that really helped my students to feel comfortable in school. (Lisa Fenton. Lisa is not a NEiTA finalist, but her insight was considered helpful.)

5

TRAINING TO BE A TEACHER

Get as much information as you can and be flexible with what you do. Talk to other teachers about how they deal with particular situations. University can give you the framework of how to teach but you have to put the bricks on. (Rebecca Armstrong. primary, government)

There are four years or more of university training required before you can become a teacher. In this section we explore some of the choices and issues involved in this training.

Education course admission

It is sometimes said that anyone can get into teaching. Clearly, that is untrue. There are several steps involved in becoming a teacher.

If you are still at school, then you will need to achieve a specified tertiary entrance score. This will vary from university to university, and from year to year, although the Commonwealth Government is moving to standardise these expectations (see Chapter 9).

The pre-requisite standards required for access to teaching courses in many universities are very achievable. However, the ease of entry belies the demands of the course, and, more significantly, the demands of teaching. Teachers must have a high level of competence in literacy and in their teaching field. In primary schools that includes mathematics and science. No matter what your teaching focus, you will need to be adept at English writing and speaking, because you cannot correct students' work with credibility if your own English writing and speaking is of a poor standard. In addition, you will need to complete a university course of study which will make demands of your English and your ability in particular areas of the curriculum, depending on the course you choose. Put simply, if you have just scraped through on a basic entry score for a teaching course, then teaching may not be an appropriate choice of course or career, or you may need to consider additional study to improve your academic standards before embarking on a teaching course.

However, failure and struggle at school can make a person an excellent teacher, because they understand the feelings and stresses of students who struggle. Unfortunately, some teachers whose own schooling was a breeze find it difficult to empathise or even understand how some students 'just don't get it', despite the teacher's efforts. If you struggled in some area of learning at school, that does not disqualify you from teaching, as long as you are aware that you will need to work hard to catch up. When you become a teacher, you can use your own school experience to relate to and help your students.

If you are entering teaching from another career, you will need to speak with the university about the entry requirements. If you already have a university degree, then you can complete either an education degree or diploma. Some universities grant entrance to students who have completed some studies as a non-university tertiary institution, such as a technical and further education (TAFE) facility, and others offer university preparation courses. There are several other options for people who do not have school graduation to enrol in an undergraduate course, so if you are keen to train as a teacher, but do not have the standard entry qualifications, do not give up; talk to the university about options. It is worth commenting that less than half of the students enrolled in teaching courses in Australian universities have come directly from school. Many will have completed an earlier degree in another discipline; some will have trained and worked as a learning assistant; many others will be mature-age students changing career. There may also be a number of international students. This mix makes for an interesting range of students who bring a variety of understandings and experiences to their studies.

Choosing a university

There are more than one hundred university campuses throughout Australia which offer teaching and/or training courses. Most of these are registered to accept international students (evident if the university has a Commonwealth Register of Institutions and Courses for Overseas Students (CRICOS) number).

A teaching course may be identified as a teaching degree (for example, Bachelor of Teaching) or, more commonly, an education degree (for example, Bachelor of Education), so, if searching online, try both fields. Courses in training generally apply to career development and continuing education and are designed for professional trainers working with adults in the workforce.

You may choose a university because it is local, because it offers a particular course, because it has a good reputation or because your friends attend there. A web search will identify the courses available at each university. Some universities within Australia are more highly reputed than others, because of their history, facilities, research achievements, quality of their courses or other factors. However, in Australia, employers are generally more impressed by the results achieved in the course than by the particular university attended. There are exceptions, and if you are ho ping to be employed by a particular school or system, you might ask them about this.

A list of Australian university education courses is found in Appendix 1.

Courses and majors

An undergraduate is someone who has not yet been awarded a degree from a university. Therefore, an undergraduate course is usually a 'first' course. When an initial degree (usually a bachelor's degree) has been completed, a student may choose to complete further or postgraduate studies — typically a graduate diploma, master's degree or doctorate. To enrol in a postgraduate course, you must already be a graduate of a university, but not necessarily the same university.

There are several options to train as a teacher:

- complete a four-year undergraduate pre-service teacher education degree, most commonly a Bachelor of Education (BEd)
- complete a Bachelor of Education and another degree at the same time; for example, a BEd and a Bachelor of Science (BSc)
- complete a three-year degree in a non-education area (for example, a BSc) and then complete a postgraduate pre-service teacher education course, most commonly a one-year Graduate Diploma in Education (DipEd).

I was inspired to enter the teaching profession after

> *completing Certificate III in early childhood, which led me to university to further my education in teaching. Whilst my time at school was largely good, for some of my peers I could see their learning styles were not being met. With that in mind I really wanted to ensure my time at university involved learning how to differentiate the curriculum and my teaching to reach all students and their learning preferences (Jenna Walsh, primary, government)*

The configurations available may vary between universities. Some people will complete further postgraduate studies before commencing their career; others will add to their qualifications by studying part-time while teaching.

Aspiring teachers can make several choices which determine the course in which to enrol.

The age of the students you hope to teach

Do you prefer to work with children aged below 8 years (early childhood), between 8 and 11 (primary school), between 12 and 16 (middle school or lower secondary school), or over 16 (upper secondary school)? These groupings are approximate, and most courses prepare teachers to teach across more than one of these age groups.

Sometimes it is useful to keep your options open. Many pre-service teachers are unsure which age group they prefer to teach until their field experience. Some are surprised that the classroom experience changes their preference significantly. In any case, versatility is valuable. You are better equipped — and your experience more appealing to an employer if you have had experience with a range of age groups. Most courses specify which levels they will qualify you to teach (BEd Secondary, DipEd Primary and so on); however, beyond these broad groupings, it will be a lottery whether you get to teach your preferred age group in your early years in the workforce. In your career, if you seek to teach a range of year levels rather than focusing too strongly on a favourite year, it will keep you fresh, challenge you and provide ongoing professional learning and development.

Most teachers of the early or primary years have completed a four-year education degree. They need a sound understanding of the complexities of teaching and learning, but not usually a great depth in any one particular learning area (such as chemistry), although the course does provide for specialisation in relevant learning areas (such as mathematics, science, English and so on). Some primary teachers have an undergraduate degree and a DipEd especially if they are teaching music, art or physical education. They may have chosen this pathway because they changed their preference from secondary to primary teaching, because they made a later decision to enter teaching, or because they had a passion for a particular learning area. However, it should be noted (at some risk of being contentious) that generalist primary teachers (that is, class teachers who teach most subjects, rather than specialising in one) whose course work in education is limited to a graduate diploma struggle with the demands of planning, assessing and teaching in the early stages of their career because they have not had the intense teacher education and field work which the four-year education degree provides.

While some secondary teachers have also completed a Bachelor of Education degree, most have completed a degree in a learning area (for example, BSc) followed by the DipEd. They do this so that they have a deep knowledge of the learning area in which they plan to teach, although their education training may be more limited. Some completed the dual degree, with a bachelor's degree in a learning area (BA, BSc, BEc, BBus, BMus and so on) completed simultaneously with a BEd.

The subject area you hope to teach

Do you prefer to work in sciences (including biology, geology, chemistry, physics), mathematics, the arts (dance, drama, music, visual art), design and technology (media, computing, business, accounting, home economics, manual arts), English, languages other than English, society and environment (social sciences, geography, economics, history), physical and health education (outdoor education, adventure education, human movement) or religious and values education? (The groupings and titles vary between universities.)

Secondary teachers are generally expected to have a depth of training in a particular field, although they may be required to teach in a 'minor' area also, depending on the size of the school and how the timetable is structured. There are also many middle schools, accommodating students somewhere between Years 5 and 10. Teachers in these schools may be required to teach subjects beyond their academic training.

In primary schools there are specialist teaching opportunities in music, art, physical education and languages. Occasionally, there are specialist appointments in science, mathematics or drama. However, because many primary schools are not large enough to support a range of 'extra' teachers, many specialist primary teachers work part-time, work across several schools or teach general class work in addition to their specialist role.

An area of educational focus

Some pre-service teachers may choose to specialise in the education of Indigenous students, students with disabilities (special education), students with learning difficulties, gifted students, library and information technologies, vocational education, English as a second language or other specific areas of educational focus. As indicated above, primary teachers in these roles may need to supplement their specialised role. This may also be true of secondary teachers in smaller schools.

Matching your interests

Your choices will determine the course you choose and the

units within that course, although there will be some units which are common to all or most courses. Not all units are available at every university, so, depending how passionate you are about your choices, you may need to shop around. As much as you are able to predict, choose a course to match your interest. You will have noted through the quotes in this book that teachers are passionate about their students' learning, and, in some cases, a particular subject area, so try to choose a course which allows you to express that passion.

> *I love music! I have some skill/talent in singing and playing instruments. I am enthusiastic ... and hopefully engaging! I love to provide ALL kids with a positive experience ... music might just be the best thing about coming to school for some kids. (Beth Wheeldon, primary, government)*

> *I chose to specialise as a business teacher because I love the world of business and finance and the thought of making money by building a successful enterprise from the ground up. Teaching was a natural extension of this passion for me, as it allowed me to share my ideas with others and innovate in new and interesting ways using their ideas. (Chris Tipper. secondary, government)*

Field work

While you can learn the theory of teaching and a depth of

subject knowledge in the university lecture theatre or tutorial, the only place to learn to teach is in the classroom. Therefore, an essential component of every education course is a classroom practicum – usually several practicums. At these times you will be placed in a classroom, initially to observe the teacher at work, and then progressively to teach the class yourself. This experience is not simply to learn to instruct students assertively, although that is a necessary skill; it is also to enable you to practise planning lessons, managing students, tailoring teaching to meet individual student needs, assessing the learning, using that assessment to inform further planning and teaching, providing feedback to students, persisting with students who struggle to learn, challenging capable students, reporting to parents, collaborating with colleagues, communicating with parents, dealing with parent concerns, and so on.

The practicum is also designed to help you understand teachers' legal responsibilities for students, the demands of staff meetings and parent interviews, the expectations of yard supervision and before and after school supervision, the expectations which the school community has of you, and the like. It is an opportunity to be supported by an experienced teacher, of whom you can ask questions, seek advice, and obtain feedback on your ideas and your practice. (Many teachers lament that, once qualified, they rarely get to see other teachers in action or to gain feedback from colleagues, because each teacher is busy in another room with their own students.)

Your mentor teachers should be able to offer suggestions and encourage you to take risks. By the end of your final practicum, you should be ready to take charge of your own classroom and should understand the expectations which come with the responsibility of being a teacher.

'Prac teachers' or 'prackies' (as they are colloquially called) are usually placed with experienced teachers who are able to supervise and mentor a trainee. However, sometimes these relationships do not work out well. It is important that each practicum is a positive experience. That will mean being flexible, showing yourself willing to listen and learn, demonstrating some humility, and making it clear that you intend to do all you can to learn as much as possible, even if you find it difficult to connect with your supervising teacher.

It is also useful to gain wide experience from the practicums. While you may see yourself as a Year r teacher, your initial appointments as a trained teacher may well be in Kindergarten and Year 3 classrooms. You could hold out for a Year 1 role, but you might find yourself unemployed for a long time! You might also find yourself allocated to a Year 3 class because the principal considers that to be the optimum matching of teachers to classes. In any case, a teacher teaches with more insight if they have a sense of how each school year level fits in the overall continuum of learning. Education begins before the child enters school and continues long after they leave Year 12. In between, learning should form a sequential continuum, not a series of unrelated one-year experiences. Therefore, seek a range of experiences in your practicums, including teaching classes you might not want to teach again.

Your practicums will assist your academic work, providing experiences on which you can base your assignments and a context to understand the theory. Be enthusiastic and open to learning, volunteer to help out and become part of the school community. Some exceptional teachers are offered their first paid teaching role in the school where they completed their final practicum, due to their performance and their commitment to their work and the school.

In order to get a job as a teacher, you will need to pass both the theory component of your course and the practical.

> *Treasure the moment of being a practicum student, because that will be one of the few times that you get to watch others teaching. Once you start teaching, you will have hardly any time to watch others teaching. It's a pity, because that's the best way to learn. (Ming Urwin, Prep to Year 12, independent)*

> *Make the most of your field experience as it's easily the most worthwhile aspect of the course. Develop strong ties with your lecturers. especially those with specific experience as teachers. Having a large group of people you know, trust and respect and who are or have been in the teaching field is very important to your own growth as a teacher. These people will support you through anything and give you critical and professional advice. (Garreth Wigg, primary, Catholic) learning*

How much work is involved in the course?

It is an interesting anomaly that a 'full-time' university course is no longer full-time! There are many students studying full-time courses and holding down part-time jobs as well.

However, a degree in teaching includes a significant practical component. Courses vary between universities, but most will require a practicum of at least a term per year. The final practicum will be assessed and your mark in this component will strongly influence your employment prospects. Many students find this practicum physically, mentally and emotionally demanding. It is not a time to try to hold down a part-time job as well. The time required for preparing and reviewing lessons (after hours) can be taxing, and comes after a day's teaching, which many prac teachers find exhausting.

> *The full degree is an opportunity to learn as much as you can. Behaviour management courses in particular are crucial to having a rewarding classroom experience. (Selena Wool, secondary, government)*

Studying part-time

Many education students study part-time and externally.

Teaching represents a career change for mature-aged people or a long-term career plan for younger students. Most units of education degrees can be completed in part-time or external modes. However, the practicum component is required of all students, so if you are in employment, you will need to take leave at these times.

While most teacher education students enter university from secondary school, teaching attracts many people who are moving from another career.

Students enrolling in initial teacher education courses form a heterogeneous cohort: Within a total of more than 70,000 students nationally, around 75 per cent are female; around 30 per cent are over 25 years of age; around 20 per cent are part-time students; around 30 per cent are international students; and Indigenous students are represented.[17] (It is the authors' opinion that the teaching profession in Australia would benefit from more Indigenous teachers and male teachers.)

Student life

Everyone experiences the student life differently. It depends on academic ability, personality, level of commitment to study and assignments, commitments beyond university (employment, family) and other factors. Universities have staff and students who will advise you about the demands and joys of university life. Because each student responds differently, some find the education degree stimulating, others find it boring; some find it very relevant, others find it less helpful.

What if I change my mind about teaching part way through the course?

Teachers learn communication skills (listening, speaking, writing, reading), organisation skills, relational skills and how to assist someone to understand and learn something. These skills are generalisable. Teachers who leave the workforce often find work as middle managers or in administration or communication roles. In addition, if you complete a pre-education degree, you will have qualifications in a subject area also, so careers which require this knowledge are also available to you.

> *I think you actually have to experience life in the classroom. There were many from my first-year uni class who dropped out after our first teaching round because they realised that it wasn't right for them. (Jodie Holman, primary, independent)*

Gaining an advantage

Many pre-service teachers develop their skills and confidence by serving as a volunteer with children or young people. This shows in their practicum, when they are more relaxed with their students and more confident in dealing with them; in their academic work, when they are able to connect the theory to their own practical experiences; and on their resume, where additional experience is usually considered favourably, because of the learning it brings and the attitude and commitment it implies.

> *There is so much more to the job than sitting in tutorials and memo rising educational theories. The passion and drive that is needed to be a part of the teaching profession cannot be taught but comes from being a part of a classroom environment. (Laura Bond, primary. government)*

> *[I would have liked] more emphasis on the 'business' of teaching not just the 'task' of teaching. In other words, teaching is not just about teaching; it's about meetings and responsibilities to keep the school functioning — all the other expectations that increase over time. (Cathy Yeoman, primary, government)*

There are many organisations which are willing to accept volunteer help — schools, child care centres, kindergartens, community and church youth and children's groups, libraries (for reading to children in vacations), after-school and holiday-care centres, sports clubs, dance schools and so on.

Some teachers in training also arrange to spend time in a

classroom at the beginning and end of the school year, when universities are in recess. These times have special demands. Beginning well may have significant impact on your first (and subsequent) years of teaching, yet it is unlikely that you will have a practicum scheduled at this time of the school year. A teacher who supervised you on a practicum, a teacher acquaintance or your local school may be happy to have you as a classroom assistant at the start or end of the year.

> *The university experience does not prepare you 100 per cent for teaching. Volunteering in a school, alongside university, will be the best foundation for entering into the teaching profession. (Sara Johns. early childhood, government)*

What won't I learn at university?

No university course can fully prepare you for the realities and practicalities of your chosen career, whatever that is. It is true of teaching too. The on-the-job experience teaches and refines our skills and knowledge. While the teaching practicum will give you an insight into the practical issues, and some experience in dealing with them, there will be some aspects that you simply will not be prepared for when you reach the classroom. It is worth noting, however, that sometimes what appears irrelevant is part of the grounding which shapes attitudes and provides a context for future learning and for teaching.

> *For me the course was nothing like the job. So much of being a teacher relies on your natural instincts, compassion, devotion and common sense. These attributes cannot be taught in a university degree. (Kate Mawson, secondary, independent)*

> *A lot of what you do in a teaching course won't be practically useful in the future (e.g. psychological theories around behaviour, very specific models for behaviour management, complex analysis of validity and reliability of assessment) but is critical for you to have an understanding of the nature of the profession. Once you begin and you're just trying to get through each lesson and each week, the teaching course will set a solid foundation for the practice of teaching, which can only really be learned by being in a classroom and then sitting down an reviewing and creating resources. Observation of experienced teachers is very valuable and should be continued beyond a training course (David Trousdell, secondary, independent)*

There are many skills that a teacher needs which are not explicitly taught at university. There are others which may be taught or experienced during the practicums, but which new teachers often find challenging.

Time management

The work of a teacher can be unending. That is, more time can always be spent profitably on better preparing lessons, developing more thorough teaching strategies for individual students, more thorough marking, personal reflection, meeting with individual students or their parents, creative collaboration with colleagues, initiating class or school events or programs. Parent meetings, reports, school events and curriculum changes do not replace the usual classroom and school responsibilities; they fit in around the usual work. Teachers need to be able to manage their time effectively.

Parent interviewing skills

It is critical that a teacher is able to communicate with parents. This involves active listening skills, responding empathetically, and speaking sensitively and assertively. Generally, this is learnt on the job and developed with one's own experience and maturity.

Negotiation skills

There is a lot of negotiation in a teacher's work – with colleagues, students and parents. Negotiation involves finding a way to work with others which meets each person's needs and goals.

Building rapport with students

At the heart of the teaching and learning process is a relationship between the teacher and student. For most children and youth, the quality of the relationship influences how well they learn.

> *Teachers take on a multitude of roles and the classroom teaching component is only a small slice. ... My first teaching appointment was in a large school and I was surprised by how much responsibility I was given as a beginning teacher. I felt quite overwhelmed at times with the workload and the expectations from senior staff members. Learning to manage my time to ensure I was planning quality teaching and learning activities along with assessments, meetings and other requirements took me longer than I anticipated. (Megan Druitt. primary, government)*

> *I was unprepared for the importance that feedback has for student achievement. Individualised feedback and differentiation in a classroom are very important, and this was not evident to me until I started. In addition. I hadn't realised the importance of students easily recognising if you liked them or not — students want to be liked and if they aren't, this can exacerbate already inherent problems. (David Trousdell, secondary, independent)*

Coping with change

Schools are places of change. At the very least, teachers need to be able to adapt to change. Ideally, they are able to facilitate change and even innovate, because successful teachers are continually searching for new and better ways to assist students as a group, and to meet the particular needs of individual students.

Managing student behaviour

Beginning teachers are often obsessed with 'control' of students. (Some experienced teachers are too.) Students do not need to be controlled; some might even say that is unethical. However, as a group, and as individuals, they need to be managed. Because they are children, their self-management skills may be limited and their judgement immature, so teachers have a duty of care toward them, as well as a need to ensure that the teaching-learning process is not disrupted.

> *The five principles which I believe are essential to being a teacher are:*
>
> 1. *It takes time to train a child*
> 2. *It takes perseverance to discipline*
> 3. *It takes wisdom to be fair*
> 4. *It takes effort to teach principles*
> 5. *It takes diligence to manage a class well. (Emily Scott-Davies, primary, independent)*

Supporting students with disabilities

Our classrooms contain many students who have diagnosed and defined disabilities, as well as many who exhibit many of the symptoms associated with disabilities, but do not have a diagnosis. Teachers need to be comfortable working with students who may be physically or intellectually impaired.

Supporting students with learning difficulties

There are also many students who struggle to learn for reasons which cannot be identified. These students are not lazy, uncooperative or lacking in effort. Despite their best and earnest efforts, some of the learning just does not 'stick'. In secondary schools, students have some flexibility to choose courses which suit their interests and abilities. In primary schools, they don't. In particular, every student must learn literacy and mathematics, no matter how difficult they find it.

If you have been a successful learner at school, you may struggle to understand why some intelligent students fail to learn effectively. You may find this frustrating, if your best efforts as a teacher fail to 'break through'. We offer you a challenge: In order to understand the frustrations for these students, the impact on their sense of self-worth, and the emotions with which they have to cope, we encourage you to attempt to learn something you find difficult. It may be playing the piano, swimming, juggling, chess or another language. Find something which you find very difficult and persist with it well beyond the point when you would like to give up — because students are not allowed to give up! This simple exercise may make you an exceptional teacher.

After graduation

When you have qualified as a teacher, you will need to apply for registration. Currently each state has its own registration body, although the Australian government is currently moving to a national registration process. The purpose of registration is to ensure that all those employed as teachers have appropriate qualifications, and a police clearance. You will be granted a 'provisional' registration while your application is being processed, but that is enough to enable you to apply for work.

6

CAREER CHOICES

School sectors

In Australia, schools can be grouped into different sectors according to their governance. In 2017, there were 9444 Australian schools, of which 70.3% were government schools and 29.7% non-government schools. Approximately 18% were Catholic, and 12% independent. Around 66% of students attend government schools, 20% Catholic schools and 14% independent schools.[18] Of course, economic and social factors cause these figures to vary marginally from year to year.

Student to teaching staff ratios vary across sectors. In government schools there were 15 students per teacher in primary schools and 12.4 in secondary schools; in Catholic schools 16.3 and 12.5; and in independent schools 14 and 10.4.

The gender split of teaching staff also varies considerably

between sectors and particularly between levels of education. In 2017, 71% of teachers were female. In primary schools 72% were female and in secondary schools 60%. Interestingly, the ratio of female teachers to male in primary schools has dropped from more than 80% in 2012, while the secondary ratio has remained the same.

Many teachers make a conscious choice to teach in the government or non-government sectors. However, there are some misconceptions promoted in the media and the community about these sectors, so the following comments offer some clarity.

Education is a state responsibility

According to the Australian Constitution, state governments are responsible for education. However, because the Commonwealth Government controls the taxation income, it can impose demands upon schools by making these matters a condition of funding. As a result, many of the regulatory requirements for schools actually come from the Commonwealth Government. This has the advantage of ensuring consistency across all states in some matters; and the disadvantage that some responses to local circumstances and local concerns are determined nationally.

All schools are subject to the same regulatory and legal expectations

Government schools are fully funded by the government, which manages buildings and staff and sets other accountabilities. In some states, principals are being given increasing authority to appoint their own staff, manage facilities and set priorities for the use of funds. Independent schools may establish their own emphases, but are regularly inspected to ensure their curriculum is appropriate, that teachers are registered, that students are achieving adequate standards, that government funding is being used appropriately for the benefit of students, and so on. Non-government schools include Catholic schools, most of which are managed by the state Catholic Education Office; and independent schools, each of which is managed by its own board, with some boards managing small systems consisting of several schools.

All schools receive government funding

All schools receive state and national funds according to a formula set out by governments. This includes non-government schools, whose parents pay taxes and are entitled to have those taxes support the education of their children. However, the government funding of each student in a non-government school is around 67 per cent of the funding provided for each student in a government school. Because teachers are paid similar salaries across all sectors, and the other costs of running a school are similar across all sectors, parents in non-government schools make up the funding shortfall by paying fees.

The ways governments fund schools will change from time to time, in response to philosophical, financial, social and political pressures. Education is an expensive item for governments, whose funds are not limitless.

Independent schools are not all wealthy schools

Despite the messages conveyed by the media, a very small percentage of non-government schools in Australia could be described as wealthy. (A small number of government schools could also be described as wealthy.) Most independent schools keep fees as low as possible, have large mortgages and make ends meet by careful governance by their boards. It is unwise to assume that if you work in an independent school you will receive a higher salary, have perfect students and unlimited resources. Each school has been established to promote a particular religious, philosophical, educational or cultural stance. If you wish to teach in a non-government school, ensure that you understand their values and expectations and are able to support these.

The issues dealt with by teachers are the same

There is more which unites teachers across the sectors than separates them. When teachers gather together across the sectors, they will talk about issues with student management, understanding curriculum, how to improve learning, the difficulties of partnering with parents and so on. Each sector conducts similar — often identical — professional learning experiences for teachers. Teaching is essentially the same in any sector, in the same way that dentistry or plumbing is the same across different employers, with dentists and plumbers undergoing similar training and similar professional learning no matter how large or small, wealthy or struggling, government or non-government, is the business for which they work — or even if they work for themselves.

However, you should also be aware that schools and systems sometimes impose limitations on the ways you teach and manage students and on the ways you express your values. Most non-government schools and systems have been founded to support a particular worldview. While no-one can tell you what to believe or think, your beliefs, scientific theories, social theories and lifestyle may not be accepted in the school, and if this is the case you will not be able to talk about them. In government schools, too, there are restrictions on what values and religious beliefs can be promoted by teachers.

> *[I chose to teach in a government school because] I wanted to support the system that supported me as a*

child and the majority of the population As a product of the public school system. it is the system that I am familiar with and believe so strongly in. I want to make a difference to all children who all have an equal opportunity. I knew public education would welcome and support me in this important step in my future. As a valued staff member I am encouraged to pursue my special interests or talents to contribute to school life — from coaching sport to coordinating a school production. With the Department of Education and Training, you are always continuing to learn. (Eliza Collings. primary, government)

Teaching in a Lutheran school gives me the opportunity to openly share my Christian beliefs with my class and their families. There is a common set of values between all stakeholders. We operate as an extended Christian family at school. (Naomi Kotzur, primary, independent)

Levels of education

Schools can be grouped according to the age of the students they teach, or the 'level' of education — primary or secondary. Within those categories, and in university courses, a distinction is often made between early childhood (commonly kindergarten to Year 2), primary school (Years 3-6), middle school (Years 7-10) and upper school (Years 11-12). (Different states have varying names for these groups.) Usually a teacher is employed as 'teacher', not as a 'Year 1 teacher' or 'English teacher' or 'Year 9 teacher'. Which year level and even which subject you teach may be influenced by your training or your preference, but will mostly be determined by which classes need to be filled. The more versatile you are the more likely you are to get work.

> *[Why choose to be a kindergarten teacher?] Knowing that I would always have a captive audience for my lame jokes and quirky behaviours'! Rewards — being front row to witnessing little steps along the way to success. Watching children grow and develop into positive community contributors, sharing in families· magic moments. Knowing you are making a difference. Difficulties — advocacy for the field and profession and recognition of its value (Tania Harrington. kindergarten. government)*

Specialist areas of teaching

Most teachers specialise to some degree. At the simplest level, trainees choose to teach early childhood, primary or secondary students. If you choose secondary teaching, you will be asked to choose a subject area or discipline in which to specialise.

You would hope to teach at the level and in the subject area for which you were trained. However, this is not always so. Sometimes, in order to get work, a secondary teacher may need to teach some classes in an area of minor specialisation. To accommodate the number of classes in (say) science, the school might need a part time (let's say, 0.6 of a full-time equivalent) science teacher. Of course, you might choose to just work 0.6 and add to your load teaching science in another school. However, the timetable may demand that your 0.6 teaching load is spread over five days, so the chances of getting work in another school where the classes dovetail neatly with your first school is highly unlikely. More typically, you would accept a full-time teaching position at the school, teaching mostly science classes, but perhaps a maths class also.

In the same way, you may be passionate about teaching Year 1 students. However, the enrolment in your school may allow for one and a half classes of Year 1 students. The school cannot afford to give you a half-class, so, more typically, you may have a class of Year 1 and 2 students together. In a country town, the class may consist of Kindergarten, Pre-Primary, Year 1 and Year 2 students!

Alternatively, you may be offered a job teaching Year 3 students, because that's where the vacancy is in the school.

The point of these examples is that, in order to obtain employment, you may need to teach outside your preferred area of specialisation. Typically, demonstrated ability as a teacher, and time in the school, give you the opportunity to negotiate a preferred role.

Over time, you may find you have an interest in an area of specialisation which you did not identify initially — in teaching struggling students or gifted students, for example. Some teachers move into a newly-found area of interest by studying part-time to gain further qualifications; others see or are given an unexpected opportunity.

> *There are many advantages of working as a business teacher, mostlv because you have the opportunity to exploit a universal appeal for all students — 'Who wants to learn how to make money?' I highly value my ability to explore financial independence with students as I strongly believe these are fundamental skills that all students need and appreciate later in their lives beyond school. (Chris Tipper, secondary. Government)*

> *1 had completed a Bachelor in Fine Art and am a practising artist. It is so very important to show students that you are passionate about your method. ... When a student completes a piece of work which they are really proud or. they come back to school and tell you that they showed their mum/dad/grandma/grandpa. This is a really rewarding feeling. Difficulties are when students are reluctant to do art because 'it's not important'. (Sarah Perry. secondary, government)*

> *I believe that Japanese is a subject that can have such a big impact on students' lives, with experiences through hosting, travel, making friends, using language, learning about a different culture and in turn their own culture, and taking those expe1iences with them into the global world they will live in. (Catherine Emmerson, secondary)*

My interest in learning enhancement (special needs education) was ignited when working in a school with a large cohort of students with learning challenges for whom I believed mainstream curriculum success was relatively unattainable. I chose to learn more about the various ways of engaging the students in my classes as well as passing on information regarding adjustments and key strategies to colleagues, particularly those in the year level I was coordinating. (Rosemary Churches, secondary, Catholic)

As a careers advisor, mentoring students and inspiring them to think about their future pathway is often challenging. I took another turn in my career when I trained long-term unemployed in communication and pre-employment skills, before I realised that teaching secondary students in careers and English may be my forte. ... I completed a Bachelor of Arts, a DipEd and a Master of Education. The skills I mostly use, though, come from previous employment prior to teaching [in training long-term unemployed to return to work]. and having a global perspective and an open mind to embrace the huge variety of opt ions students now have. (Chloe Hofman. secondary, independent)

Teachers in specialist areas often find that their subject is not given the same respect as 'core' subjects (English, mathematics, science, society and environment); that they struggle to maintain sufficient classes to work full—time in one school; and that the subject may demand a great deal of out of school time for rehearsals, performances, displays, fixtures, carnivals and so on.

However, it is worth noting that schools usually value and try to make use of teachers with a high level of expertise in an area — as long as that expertise includes being an expert teacher, not just having expert knowledge!

Teaching adults

Teaching adults is a different area of specialisation. If teaching adults is something you wish to pursue then these courses are often provided through university business faculties as training and development degrees. However, teaching of children and youth is an excellent foundation for teaching adults.

Career paths to leadership

There are many opportunities for promotion in secondary schools, but typically far fewer in primary schools, although this imbalance is shifting slowly. Promotion is usually by application, often to a different school.

Leadership positions are not escape routes for those who are tired of the classroom. Promotion is by merit, so you will need to show expertise as a teacher and experience in leadership. That sounds like a cart before the horse, but the reality is that to prove your readiness for 'formal' leadership you should demonstrate successful experience in 'informal' leadership.

If you aspire to formal leadership, you can showcase your talents by taking on volunteer leadership roles. Don't do it just to score points; if you have a passion for leadership, these roles should come naturally to you. People suited to leadership tend to find that, despite being busy with a regular teaching load, they find themselves noticing opportunities for improving the school management, curriculum or extracurricular programs. You might, for example, have ideas for a program to combat cyber-bullying or engage students in leadership or critical thinking.

Don't wait for someone to tap you on the shoulder; instead, be proactive and approach the school leadership team with your ideas. Or, simply approach the leadership team to express your willingness to help out with whatever needs to be done. There are many opportunities in schools for teacher s to volunteer for minor leadership roles, such as leading or participating in organising events, assisting with school planning, reviewing programs or overseeing change implementation. Your willingness to lead will be appreciated and noted by those in management, and in time may result in more formal leadership responsibilities being offered to you.

You should choose leadership because you want to make a difference. Leadership is not simply a natural progression for a teacher; nor a reward for longevity; nor a right or entitlement.

Successful leaders articulate clear reasons why they chose to seek leadership opportunities and why they continue in leadership.

Good teachers don't automatically make good leaders. School leadership requires different skills from teaching, so the development of these skills is essential if you aspire to leadership. In addition to gaining experience in minor leadership roles, you might complete postgraduate qualifications. Further study enables you to show understanding of current issues and developments, and demonstrates a desire to keep learning. Some postgraduate courses involve action research – practice-based research which you conduct in your own school or classroom. Conducting action research within your school in order to answer real problems which your school has articulated is also useful background to leadership.

However, you should be aware that there may be limitations to your eligibility for leadership in the non-government sector. Because Catholic and independent schools have mostly been established to promote a particular religious, philosophical or education al perspective, the school may appoint as leaders only those who are genuinely committed to that perspective.

> *It's a great way to be able to make a difference. Being a principal gives you the chance to create a vision for a school and to make a real difference to kids. Start planning early. Keep a logbook of the things you do and the professional development you have engaged in.*

(Christine Hills, principal, primary, government)

Go for it. Try to become a well-rounded individual and to think strategically about where you put your efforts. Does taking the school netball or football team really demonstrate your ability to lead a school as both a curriculum and instructional leader1 Would you be better off undertaking some data analysis or leading a curriculum team? (Jedda McNeill, principal, primary, government)

Your role as principal is to lead. inspire, support and guide the school community towards the achievement of its goals. It is a multifaceted role that will require a level of commitment and dedication that some people are unable to sustain. Be prepared to be the 'meat in the sandwich' on occasions between parents and teachers, so learn to be a good mediator. Essentially though. never lose sight of why you became a teacher, because the same reasons should drive you as you become a principal. (Kim Doust, principal. primary. government)

7

EMPLOYER EXPECTATIONS

We want the whole package — someone who understands curriculum as well as how to deal with students and parents; someone who has strong interpersonal skills with other adults; someone who can take direction but who can also show initiative; someone with computer skills; someone who is not content with the status quo, but who can work within it. (Jedda McNeill, principal, primary, government)

Obtaining a job as a teacher is one thing; keeping it another; and thriving in it is different again. In this section we explore the expectations that employers will have of you.

The job market for teachers varies from time to time. In addition to the new graduates and immigrants who add to the supply of teachers each year, there is also a large pool of teachers who do not have permanent employment, but are keen to work year by year. Earlier, we discussed how to give yourself the best chance of being employed. But, once in the school, what will your principal expect of you?

Putting students first

Schools exist for students — not to provide employment for teachers nor childcare for parents. Students come first. There are times when teachers would like all students to just go away, if only long enough for the teacher to have an uninterrupted coffee; when what is right for students is not very right for teachers; when teachers are pushed beyond their comfort zone to learn new ways of teaching which benefit students; and when events which enrich the life and experience of students add to teachers' workloads. In a school, students come first, and that places demands on teachers' time and attitudes.

> *I expect my teachers to have the kids as their number one focus and, with everything they do. pose the question ·is this in the best interest of the children I am teaching? If not. why am I doing it?' I expect teachers to be caring and compassionate while setting high standards for their class. (Des Deighton, principal, primary. government)*

> *Go into your classroom willing to participate in a partnership. I know that I come into the classroom with a set of knowledge, but my students also come into the*

classroom with knowledge. I find that I impart knowledge in the process but I also gain knowledge. I don't presume to know everything. but share what I know. I also invite my students to share what they know and, in doing so, I find that the teaching and learning environment becomes an equal participation — a 'dance' if you will ... sometimes, an intense paso doble and other times a swooning waltz, often simply a joyous frolic ... but always a dance that involves both partners — me and my students. And that 'dance' is defined by a shared conversation and shared learning. (Sophie Fenton, secondary. independent)

Responsibility

Most students in schools are children, in legal definition, so they require care. Supervising students is a responsibility which can result in legal action if neglected. The principal must be confident that teachers know what is expected of them and will carry it out without close supervision.

As a student, you may have felt that you were over-supervised, with teachers seeming to watch your every move. As a teacher, of course, you will not experience the same level of scrutiny. However, the expectations are high. For much of the day, you will be responsible for the management, safety, wellbeing and education of a group of students, most of whom will be legally classified as minors. You cannot leave them to their own devices while you finish a cup of coffee, chat with a colleague, make a phone call or think about what you will do in the lesson. If accidents happen, if students get into a fight, if students are not learning as well as they should, if students are disrupting the learning of other classes or those within the class, or if you are not performing with the skill and maturity expected of a teacher, you will be called to account.

Continual learning

Your university education is the start of your professional learning journey. Throughout your career you will be expected to keep learning. That will involve participation in professional learning required by your employer, professional reading and learning at your own initiative, and, ideally, continuing postgraduate studies. Evidence of continuing learning is essential for continued registration as a teacher, which is essential to allow you to teach. In any case, teaching is a learning profession. You cannot be committed to learning for others (that is, for students) and not be committed to your own learning.

> *It is important to know that having achieved your teaching degree is not enough to prepare you for being a teacher. You must commit yourself to being a lifelong learner; learning from postgraduate courses, attending professional development opportunities. from widely*

> *reading and from ether staff. You can never afford to be comfortable. You must be open to change and new ideas and prepared to adjust your thinking, as times or circumstances demand of you. (Lyn Miller, early childhood. government)*

At the time of your graduation as a teacher, you will have achieved graduate-level skills as defined by the Australian Professional Standards for Teachers. In an earlier section, we summarised the array of skills which teachers draw on in their work, and which need to be developed. In addition, a teacher's knowledge is continually evolving in certain areas, such as these:

- How people learn. How does the brain function when it is learning? What strategies can a teacher use to maximise the learning of each student? How do people differ in the ways they learn? How can the teacher recognise these differences? Interestingly, recent developments in medical technology have enabled rapid gains in the study of neuroscience and how people learn. It is difficult for teachers to keep abreast of this research.

- How to address the social and emotional needs of students and the impact of society on these. Currently, teachers need to keep up to date with the impact of electronic social media, their application to cyber-bullying, communication skills and engagement, and the impact of computers and media on the development of the young. Additionally, while much of the development of children and youth is in-built and therefore unchanged across time and place, some aspects of development may be brought about by changes in nutrition, the social and cultural environment and other influences.

- Teaching and learning technologies. There is a continual evolution of learning technologies with the potential to support learning, and teachers' knowledge and use of these must be current.
- Changes to the content of the subjects being taught. Scientific knowledge is growing rapidly; the content of geography, history and economics subjects is constantly changing; mathematics is an evolving discipline. No teacher can expect to teach forever — or even for 10 years — based on what they learnt at university.
- Changes to government rules and regulations. State and Commonwealth governments regularly make decisions that teachers need to understand and implement.

Hours beyond the work day

When we asked teachers what they thought someone considering teaching should know, probably the most dominant response was that teaching is not a nine to five job. Before students arrive and/or after they leave, teachers are expected to be available for meetings with parents and colleagues, to participate in co-curricular activities, and more. In addition, teachers must prepare for lessons, mark work, complete reports, stay up to date with professional reading, attend to administrative responsibilities, read communications and so on, after hours and perhaps at home.

There are professions in which employees are paid overtime rates at busy times and even bonuses. The education industry is not one of these. In addition to the normal work beyond the school day, there are peak times – when reports or teaching programs are due, when a new curriculum is being implemented, when parent meetings or interviews are required. There are also some troughs, especially in secondary schools during exam times or after senior students have left school. A teacher's year is considered to be 48 weeks, although students are present for only 40 of those weeks, and teacher s are not normally required to be at school for all 48 weeks. So the 'overtime' evens out over time.

Going the extra mile

Schools are lean organisations. They do not have dedicated staff to deal with each task that needs attention. Schools function as communities, where people step in to do what needs to be done. Principals expect staff to contribute to the school, not just by doing a good job in the classroom, but also by volunteering for the extra things which enrich the learning or the school community.

Teachers volunteer to assist with the graduation ceremony, sports carnivals, book week, the Anzac Day service, school anniversary celebrations, sporting teams, cultural activities, drama performances, clubs, the yearbook, fundraising for charities, curriculum reviews, policy or procedural reviews, student leadership and so on. Of the many things you recall happening in the life of your school, beyond the classroom teaching, most were probably organised or supervised by teacher volunteers. While responsibility for some of these things may be allocated to particular staff, these people often do not have the time or resources to do these things themselves; their role may be to oversee them, and they will require further staff volunteers to assist. You may observe some teachers who volunteer willingly to assist with these things, because they find that their participation, while an extra load, enriches their lives, as well as enriching the school community.

When an unexpected event or emergency takes a teacher away from a class, someone must step in, because students cannot be left unsupervised. So principals also expect teachers to volunteer, or to act without complaint to supervise a class, if they happen to be free and a colleague has taken ill, been delayed in a parent interview, is attending to a student emergency or is unavailable for some other reason.

Standards of behaviour and performance

Teachers are in a key position of influence on the young. Teachers do not just teach subjects; they teach impressionable children and young people. Students are the content of teaching as much as science or mathematics are. Students learn their values and behaviour from the significant adults in their lives, and teachers are among those significant adults.

This requires high standards of behaviour and performance — perhaps higher than teachers might normally expect of themselves. Like it or not, teachers are role models for the students in their care. When that role modelling fails to meet the standards expected by parents, colleagues or the principal, the teacher will be questioned.

Teaching is a communication process; it is built on trust and respect and relationship. Children and youth have very fine-tuned sensors for hypocrisy and injustice. Teachers who set standards for students which they do not achieve themselves very quickly lose respect — and their effectiveness as teachers.

In a practical sense, this means that if students are required to dress to a particular standard, then the teacher's dress standard must be at least as high as that demanded of students; if students are expected to speak to teachers with respect and courtesy, then teachers must model that in speaking to students; if students are expected to always be prepared for class, and to have completed assigned work, then teachers must ensure that they are prepared for class, and meet deadlines , including those promised to students, such as return of marked work; if students are expected to present well-written work, teachers must ensure that their own written material — notes, tests, letters to parents and so on — models the standard of writing expected; if students are expected to maintain an organised workbook, show good time management and learn organisational skills, teachers must model similar skills.

What a teacher does at a nightclub on Saturday night, how they behave outside school hours, matters. Online social media present a particular problem. Some schools have a documented policy which forbids teachers from 'friending' students on interactive websites or posting photos or comments which reflect poorly on themselves or their school. Teachers' behaviour outside work or online that brings the school into disrepute or damages parents' confidence in a teacher or the school may be grounds for termination. You may argue that what you do in your own time is your business, but that simply is not so. Parents have a right to choose which adults influence their children and to expect certain standards of those they cannot choose. The school needs enrolments, so if parents withdraw their children because of the staff, that damages the school's future. In any case, a teacher cannot succeed without respect and credibility in the eyes of students, so any action which destroys that respect impairs the teacher's effectiveness.

Teachers are expected to exhibit the qualities we expect in students, such as integrity; honesty; a commitment to justice whether we 'like' a person or not; respect — for those in positions of authority, for peers, for those we lead or supervise or teach; courtesy; empathy; perseverance and so on.

These qualities are not show qualities; they cannot be faked. Teachers are not people who play a role and pretend to be good people. Students want to be taught by real people, whose experiences and emotions are authentic and honest, but whose lives are underpinned by sound values and personal qualities.

> *The responsibility that comes with teaching is massive. You are in charge of young minds and hearts that see you as a role model and in some cases young minds that place you on the 'I want to be like that person' ladder. You must search your soul and know you were made for teaching. It's not just a job but a vocation. (Robyn Fitzgerald, early childhood/primary, Catholic)*

> *Commitment: To students. to other teachers. to families. to do the best job you possibly can. We ask this of our students, we should expect nothing less from ourselves. (Meredith Dick, director, early childhood, government)*

Transitions and follow-up

There are many jobs in which you leave the job behind when you leave work. Teaching is not one. A teacher cannot simply walk into a classroom and decide what to do. It requires preparation. In some roles, particularly in secondary schools, there is a pattern or cycle of lessons, which enables some preparation to transfer from one class to the next, even one year to the next. In a primary classroom, more preparation is required by way of practical learning resources and planning for individual needs. The balance is that secondary teachers often have marking to do after lessons, whereas most primary teachers provide feedback to students on the spot. This is not because they don't want to mark work after hours, but because feedback is far more effective, especially with primary students, if it is immediate.

In addition, what is difficult to explain to anyone who is not a teacher is that students worm their way into a teacher's mind. When not at work, teachers often find themselves thinking about their students: How can I help Zac, who is disengaged? What can I do for Jane, who is living in difficult circumstances 1 How can I get Kalinda to see that she has the ability to go on to tertiary studies? How can I get James to learn to read. The thoughts go on. They intrude even when the teacher thinks they have left work behind.

> *Teaching is an extremely rewarding profession but you have to be passionate about working with children and meeting their needs, patient and prepared to put in the time. Teaching is not a 9:00 to 3:00 job, but it is a career that keeps on giving if you put in the time and effort. (Veronica MacNeil, primary, government)*

Critical reflection

Reflective practice is a process by which we think about how our actions impact on others and how their actions and other factors are impacting on ours. In the context of teaching, we reflect on how we connected with the students, how they understood what we were teaching them , and the degree to which our teaching and learning strategies succeeded in this lesson with these students.

We also reflect on how we responded to a disruptive student — did our response help the student to reflect on their own behaviour, did it minimise the disruption to the learning of other students, did it maintain our relationship with the disruptive student and other students?; or how we responded to the insightful and challenging question from a bright student; or how we will follow up this lesson, given what we observed about the level of understanding of the concepts explored in this lesson.

And we reflect on the assumptions behind our actions: is my frustration with this particular class affecting my teaching and their attitude to the learning; is my teaching style appropriate; in parent interviews am I coming across as arrogant, assuming that I know more than the parents about this child?

To be critically reflective means to be constantly reflecting on our work and considering how we might do it better. It is living a fundamental assumption that I cannot control the thoughts or actions of others, but I can manage my own thoughts and actions, and can ensure that I do everything I can to keep learning and growing and performing as well as I am able.

> *The greatest gift in life is to be in the position to be able to give and to be of service. Teaching is about trying to be the best teacher you can be. One must reflect on his or her performance and identify areas that need improvement. Aiming to be a better teacher each term is also paramount. (Peter Williamson, primary, independent)*

Relationship building

There is an adage which says, 'I don't care how much you know until I know how much you care.' A teacher 's effectiveness is greater when they have a rapport with their students. A teacher will be less effective if they expect to walk into a classroom, deliver a lesson and walk out, avoiding their students until the next lesson. In any case, the goals of education refer to more than intellectual knowledge. They include reference to emotional and social development. The Commonwealth Government's stated goals for education are (1) that Australian schooling promotes equity and excellence and (2) that all young Australians become successful learners, confident and creative individuals and active and informed citizens.[19]

Schools are less like organisations and more like communities, because their operation, and the conduct of the people within the school, is premised more on relationships than roles. Teachers are motivated largely by the sense of personal satisfaction they get from helping students to learn and succeed. Students may be more motivated by engaging teachers than by any innate joy in the subject matter itself. Young people are likely to be drawn to, enjoy and succeed in classes in which they feel a rapport with the teacher.

> *Learning to be a great teacher is about learning to love working with young people, particularly those who don't fit your stereotypical profile of a 'good student' These are the ones who will need you most' (Chris Tipper. secondary, government)*

Collaboration

Teachers need to be willing to work with others — to be willing to share ideas, and to collaborate to plan, review and solve problems.

This is almost a contradiction to the nature of teaching. Teachers spend a great deal of time in a classroom, working alone with a group of students. They are, for much of the day, almost their own boss. Yet, increasingly, teachers must seek ways to collaborate with others in planning, reviewing and even teaching.

Collaboration allows a student to move from year to year with a seamless and sequenced transition. Teachers who do not collaborate have no idea what the teacher before them has taught, and no idea of what the teacher in the following year will teach. The consequence for the children is lack of consistency, gaps in learning and difficulty in making the connections from one year to the next. It is important that teachers engage in reflective dialogue in order to support learning for each student.

> *Some advice to a n aspiring teacher would be to learn to collaborate and work with colleagues. parents and other professionals as pan of a team of people that help to teach and shape your students to achieve their full potential. You don't have to do it all by yourself. (Grace Vagliviello, primary, Catholic'.*

Support for school values and culture

Culture is critical. Students learn values, behaviours, social and emotional skills far more through the school culture than they do through lessons. Multiple lessons about respect, for example, will not teach students as effectively as the role modelling of their teacher and other members of the school community. In addition, the culture determines the way staff members relate to one another, to students and to parents, and influences the ways that parents relate to staff.

While the nuances of culture will vary from school to school, there is a framework of values which underlies the culture of all Australian schools.

> *[School leaders expect] that teachers endorse a whole school culture that is based upon the principles of inclusiveness. acceptance of difference and enthusiastic participation. (Ann Hardy, secondary, government)*

> *Principals expect that teachers uphold the same school values that children are also expected to adhere to. Teachers are expected to be supportive role models for children and be positive facilitators of all aspects of learning. (Julie Blyth, primary. government)*

Passion and commitment

All of the above are important. Yet the qualities most desired and expected by employers or principals are passion and commitment. They want teachers who want to be in the classroom, who are passionate about student learning, who share the excitement of the student in their success. They want people who will teach not just with intellect, but also with heart.

> *Principals and leaders expect teachers to be passionate about what they do. Thev want their staff to be organised, demonstrate initiative and work collaboratively in a team.*

It is also important that teachers are critically reflective about their teaching practice and incorporate new and innovative ideas into their teaching. Do not choose to do teaching because you 'didn't know what else to do'. Choose to do teaching because you are passionate about it. Enjoy having a positive impact on young people and want to make a difference to future generations. (Laura Clements, primary, government)

It is important that new teachers are flexible, enthusiastic, demonstrate initiative and have a general desire to work with children for their social, emotional and educational benefit. (Damien Greig, principal. primary, government)

8

SECRETS OF SUCCESS

Heart. Pure and simple. It has to come from there. With heart comes relationships — with children, with families, with colleagues. It's only with these relationships that true success as a teacher comes. With heart comes passion — it's the joy in doing something you love and making a difference. With heart comes belief — the belief that all children are competent individuals with rights, amazing capabilities and creativity, and a sense of wonder in the world. (David Gilkes, early childhood, government)

In the previous section, we explored the expectations of employers. Meeting their expectations is essential to succeed. In this section we explore other things you might do to ensure success as a teacher.

For most teachers, the decision to become a teacher is about wanting to make a difference. Successful teachers avoid being distracted by the politics, administrative demands and other frustrations associated with their work; instead they retain a focus on their students, always seeking the best for them. They ensure that they are driven not just by the intellect, but also by the heart.

> *I don't feel there is a secret success formula to being a teacher, however I strongly believe now more than ever that you have to love the job. The time spent in the classroom each day with my students is what gets me out of bed every morning (Loreta Fin, Prep to Year 12, independent)*

Of course, every year brings new students and new challenges, so it is important to reflect often and look for ways to constantly review, refine and renew 1 That includes the following.

Know yourself

Before you can understand others you must first understand yourself. What motivates you, what stresses you, what are your coping mechanisms, what things 'press your buttons' and how do you respond to them? Knowing yourself and how to manage yourself is critical in developing strong and positive relationships with your students, including those whose behaviour is challenging. Many behavioural issues are escalated by the reaction of the teacher. Successful teachers are able to reflect critically on their own performance and responses.

The best advice I could offer an aspiring teacher is to be yourself. ...Trying to teach to your own style and endeavouring not to teach too much is important. Enjoying the constant engagement you have with children is very rewarding — we can learn a great deal from them. (Peter Williamson, primary, independent)

Make a commitment to yourself and your students to be the best teacher you possibly can. Never underestimate your influence. You may be that one special person who sees and believes in a child's potential. I learning is a flame, as a teacher you have the power to either ignite it with your enthusiasm or douse it with your apathy. (Ann Newton, early childhood, government)

Know your stuff

That does not mean that a teacher has to be the 'font of all knowledge'. In today's world, students will often know things the teacher doesn't. Rather, it means understanding how to guide students' thinking in a way which takes them logically from what they know to what they don't, and which enables you to challenge each student's thinking.

There are basic fundamentals that a teacher requires for success — they need to know their material, know their students and love being in the educational space. (Sophie Fenton, secondary, independent)

A teacher should not set out to be inspirational, but rather be passionate about what they teach. Students sense passion. and passion inspires, (Rod Sheehan. secondary, Catholic)

Know your students

The first step in any learning should be to know your students. Take an interest in their abilities, struggles, interests and the ways their brains work.

Students learn better from someone they respect and with whom they have a rapport However, it is important to be an adult to your students. Some teachers begin their career not much older than their students. It is easy to confuse the relationship, and once boundaries are crossed it is difficult to go back. Even teachers of young children sometimes seek to be a fun-loving friend, rather than a teacher. Developing relationships is important, but the relationship is that of an adult, a teacher, not a best mate.

Teachers need passion. enthusiasm and an ability to not only fill students' minds with knowledge but to be able to guide and support them through their many journeys they will share with you. Teachers need to get to know their students and allow them to know you. as positive teacher-student relationships are essential to ensure that students are happy and engaged at school. (Megan Ross. primary. government)

The secret to success as a teacher is to believe in the child and that children want to learn. Success is achieved through respect. flexibility, integrity and real understanding of what the individual needs as a learner. (Yvonne Rinaldi, principal, primary, independent)

Prepare

Preparation is essential. You cannot succeed as a teacher if you are unprepared, making it up as you go along. Of course, flexibility matters — being able to adapt your plans to the responses of students and to the myriad unexpected things that can happen during a lesson; but those who are most able to adapt are those who are well prepared.

Preparation is the key! Be organised, confident and have plenty of activities for the children to do. Before you graduate, use any spare time you may have to volunteer at a variety of different schools. You will learn a lot working in different environments. (Des Deighton, principal, primary, government)

Begin well

Thorough preparation gives you the best chance to begin well. Many new teachers have difficulties in their first year because they fail to establish clear and appropriate expectations and then struggle to retrieve the situation.

Principals also advocate preparing by getting to know the school and community in which you will be working. The purpose is not to make negative judgements, but to understand the emphases and core values of the school, the aspirations and values of the local community, and the characteristics of the students you will be teaching.

- *Read as much information as you can about the service in which you will be working.*
- *Research the community and needs of the children in that community.*
- *Speak to other teachers before you commence, to gather information.*
- *Know your content.*
- *Be prepared to make mistakes and to try again — evaluate and re-do things a better way.*
- *Be well prepared — organise your day ahead so that everything is at your fingertips. (Lyn Best, director, early childhood, community preschool)*

No matter how thorough the preparation, there will be times when you are faced with information overload. It is essential to be organised and to have in place strategies to process, retain and be able to locate this information.

> *I was overwhelmed with information and would very easily misplace notices from meetings and forget things told to me. So, be organised. Create a to-do list and note down every job that you need to do, big or small. Cross*

off each job as you do it. Keep different folders, clearly labelled, to put in different notices/handouts and so on; for example: staff meetings, planning meetings, committee meetings and so on. (Elise Butters, primary, government)

Engage students in the learning

People learn when they are engaged. When you cease to be engaged in this book you will put it down, literally or mentally. Your students will do the same with your lesson. Seek ways to engage them in the learning.

However, students will not learn effectively simply by being busy doing things. While students may learn new things independently and may use activity to practise or apply learning, the teacher still has a critical role to play — not just standing at the front, instructing, but also questioning and challenging the thinking of individual students while moving around the classroom.

Plan intentionally to maximise learning opportunities for children All children are unique individuals. They learn in different ways and at different rates. The learning experiences offered to children should reflect this diversity so that you set children up for success. Differentiation is the key to success. (Tina Wilson, early childhood/ primary, government)

Make parents your allies

The students are not your children. They are given in trust by the parents. No matter how caring a person you are, a student's parents have a greater emotional commitment to the child than you. They also know them far more thoroughly than you can ever do. What you offer is an understanding of child and youth development, knowledge of how people learn, and knowledge about how the student interacts in a classroom setting. So avoid approaching parents with a view to telling them what they should do; rather, share your concerns, pool your knowledge, and find joint solutions that are reinforced at home and school.

Teachers sometimes assume that parents know what is going on at school, what the teacher is trying to do and what their expectations are of students. However, logically, they won't know these things unless you have explained them, and, even then, they may have forgotten or misunderstood. Ensure parents are informed, as a group and individually. Difficult conversations with parents are often about surprises – presenting the parent with information which they had no inkling of. Be careful to not be an alarmist and overreact to situations. Parents don't respond well to unexpected bad news where children are concerned. So, where possible, ensure parents are aware of your emerging concerns and communicate unexpected news sensitively. Treat parents as partners in the education journey.

I was least prepared for the very wide scope of the role of a teacher — not only encompassing the teaching and learning aspect but peacemaking, negotiating, consoling. counselling, boosting self-esteem, instilling values and respect and not only with students but parents as well. (Susan Keith, Prep to Year 12, Catholic)

Find mentors among your colleagues

It is also important to develop sound relationships with colleagues, which will enable you to fee l you belong and provide you with personal and professional support as necessary.

Teaching can be isolating work. Typically, a teacher spends a large part of his or her time as the only adult in a classroom of children or youth. Even if other adults are present, they may interact very little, except in relation to the work. Teachers tend to extend that way of working to other aspects of their work — planning lessons, marking, deciding how to deal with a difficult student, meeting with parents, handling the paperwork, writing reports and so on. When pressure mounts, many teachers tend to withdraw further, embarrassed to admit that they may be having difficulties coping, either with students or the teaching or the paperwork. If they are not observed in their work by peers or school leaders, it may be that nobody notices until a critical incident occurs — the teacher yells at a student, a key deadline is missed, the teacher is rude to a parent.

There is a huge amount of on-the-job learning for a teacher. Most teachers need help through the early stages. Bravado is not necessary. Most teachers understand what a new teacher is going through, and are very willing to offer advice. There is also a great deal of unwritten routine in a school – things that happen, implicit expectations – which you may not know about until it's too late. Determine to seek support from your colleagues. Admit when it is becoming difficult and ask for advice.

It might be helpful to identify two mentors. One mentor should have experience, maturity, wisdom and a willingness to be a listening ear. They do not have to be someone you envisage becoming a best friend, nor do they have to be teaching in your faculty or area; they do, however, need to be willing to offer advice when asked, to allow you to honestly talk through a situation that has arisen and to help you to find a way to deal with it. The other mentor should teach in a similar year level or subject area to you. What you want from them is to keep you ahead of expectations: what events are coming up, what are you expected to do, what deadlines must be met, what are the pitfalls, who do you defer to in this matter? When you have identified these people, explain to them what you want of them and ask for their help.

> *Work with a quality mentor. There is a lot to absorb in the first few years of your career that you will not learn from a book. A mentor will help you to blend what you have learnt and put it into effective practice. It's about*

working smarter, not harder. A mentor can guide and support you while providing constructive feedback. (Tina Wilson, early childhood, government)

Choose a mentor. Your mentor should act as your guide and your measuring stick. Observe others and pick all of the 'best bits' — the bits that work for you. Accept advice as a small gift and model your work on cobbled together 'best bits'. (Robert McPherson, primary, government)

Stay fresh

As with any job, there can be a sense of the mundane to teaching. Day by day, you interact with the same students; year by year you may teach similar content to similar students, and deal with similar issues. However, teachers are working with people, and each person is unique. Each offers his or her unique personality, interests, character, struggles and aspirations. Each needs to be treated as an individual — as we expect people to treat us.

The demands of teaching are relentless, but successful teachers find ways to re-energise themselves. This might mean teaching a different year level, moving to a different school, teaching in a different sector, trying a new teaching strategy, accepting a new challenge or responsibility, enrolling for further study, volunteering for committees, conducting research in the school, participating in an international exchange program, and so on.

Maintain a work-life balance

In any job, it is important to maintain a work-life balance. Teachers often find that difficult, because teaching can be all-encompassing. Some teachers deal with this by working a full day, so that they don't have to take work home. They might work 6.30 a.m. to 4.30 p.m. or 8.00 a.m. to 6.00 p.m., and only at peak times, such as reporting or planning, do they take work home. Others find themselves drained at the end of the day, so prefer to go home and relax, then work in the evening. Family and friends matter and ought not to be neglected, so teachers need to adjust their work times to fit with their partner's work times or the needs of children.

A further need is to let students go emotionally. A teacher cannot help but be affected by the emotional stresses of their students, and the physical, mental and emotional strain of a day's teaching on themselves. However, successful teachers find a way to 'vent' that emotion, with exercise, for example, or connecting with a friend, and then try to put the students' needs out of their mind until the next day. It is necessary to be empathetic to students and sensitive to their issues; however it is neither necessary nor heal thy to take their emotional issues upon yourself. Successful teachers find ways to deal with stress, to handle waking in the middle of the night, and to clear their heads of the burdens of all of their students.

They also ensure that family and friends understand the

demands of their work. Sometimes teachers find themselves in conflict with their partners because of the need to bring work home or because they find it difficult to clear their mind of the day's issues. Some teachers get home and say 'No marking tonight.' Others get home and say 'No dinner tonight'. Ensure your partner or family understand, seek their patience at difficult times and ask them to tell you when you appear distracted.

> *I set myself goals and time limits. I make sure l prioritise my commitments. Family comes first; my career is important but my role as a mother takes precedence over everything. Organisation is the key, but you have to be able to identify your own imbalances before you can achieve a work-life balance. (Heather Collin, primary, government)*

> *Every day is a new adventure. You need to have the ability to let things go at the end of one day and be able to start afresh the next. You also need to be able to know when to switch off. (Teacher, secondary, government)*

9

THE FUTURE OF TEACHING

I am very excited about how information and communication technology is being used to support student learning. … ICT instantly engages students and used with other learning activities has the potential to make learning meaningful. (Lyn Miller, earlv childhood/special education, government)

We have described a range of things you might want or need to know to decide whether to enter teaching or to prepare for teaching as a career. However, you are considering a career not for the present, but the future. In this section we explore some future trends which may impact on your career as a teacher.

There is no shortage of writers who theorise about the future of education – including us! Some of these focus on the goals of schooling, some on industrial issues facing teachers, some on the impact of new technologies, some on social changes. One educator and policymaker outlines 10 propositions for the future of education:

- that student engagement will continue to be a strong determining factor in relation to individual student achievement and overall school performance
- that bullying behaviour will continue to be an area where teachers will have to be vigilant
- that the provision of appropriate support for students with special needs and meeting the aspirations of their parents will continue to challenge schools and education systems
- that local and global issues will be incorporated into the content of the curriculum in schools
- that the human resources units of education systems will adjust their policies to better match the preferences of teachers for work- life balance
- that some current technology tools will become mainstream, some that are popular today will soon become obsolete and new technologies will emerge
- that the physical environment of schools will develop to enable more flexible uses of community resources
- that the similarities between government schools and non-government schools will become more apparent than their differences

- that a number of the programs and services provided by individual schools will be steered by parents as schools are increasingly seen as social networking sites
- that schools' duty of care to children will increase.[20]

> *[What excites me about the future of teaching is] that children never cease to amaze me with their capabilities and that I get to be a part of helping each child I teach become a functioning independent member of society. [I'm also excited] that through technology that is in the classroom, the only limit is my imagination. (Tina Tilbee, early childhood, government)*

Technology

Digital information and communication technologies have changed teaching. As a vehicle for learning, the power of computers is constantly evolving. We have almost unlimited access to almost unlimited information. Children and youth are among the early adopters of new technologies. Schools cannot avoid using technologies to engage students, nor should they ignore the technological skills which students bring to the classroom.

No-one can be certain how technology will evolve. Current discussions in schools tend to focus on questions such as:

- How can we use information and communication

technologies (ICT) to enhance learning?

- What devices should we use?
- How can we provide these for students?
- How can we monitor student use?
- How can we limit inappropriate use of technology, such as cyber-bullying?
- How can we discern individual work from work created by or with others?

In a decade, these questions may be redundant. Who knows what questions will vex teachers then? Perhaps:

- How can we monitor students who are working at home or at some other site?
- How can we monitor the quality of the curriculum each student has planned for himself or herself?
- How can we encourage better collaboration by students and teachers, and less personal ownership of work?

What we can predict with some confidence is that JCT will play an increasing role in education and that teachers who are confident to explore and experiment with new technologies will be valued.

As a science teacher the opportunities that new technologies have opened up for research and communication are now very accessible. This has helped more teachers and students find a passion for learning that should continue into the future. (Leslie White. secondary, government)

> *Possibilities with technology excite me about the future of teaching Five years ago I didn't have an interactive whiteboard; now not only do I rely on it, but my kids wirelessly hook up to 1t through laptops and tablets. The possibilities are endless. (Melissa Bennett, primary. government)*

Governmental directions

Education in Australia has been going through a revolution in an effort to create a national platform for quality in education. The Commonwealth Government has established the Australian Institute of Teaching and School Leadership (AITSL) to lead the work in improving teacher quality through a number of reforms, including those listed below.

Australian Professional Standards for Teachers

The standards represent a statement about what teachers do in the 21st century. This is the first time the country has created a national professional standard, which will be used to improve teacher quality. The national professional illustrations of practice provide additional tools for teachers to engage with the standards. Video clips demonstrate the standards in a range of contexts and phases of schooling, provide a basis for teachers to begin conversations around what the standards mean and look like, and assist teachers to reflect on their practice.

Nationally consistent pre-service education

Until recently, the variance in teacher education programs around the country has led to inconsistencies in standards. However, a national approach to pre-service education has resulted in universities around the country reviewing teacher education programs to ensure they align to the Australian Professional Standards for Teachers. This enables new teachers to graduate from university achieving a specified minimum standard, known as the graduate standard.

Nationally consistent teacher registration

All teachers in Australia must be registered to teach. In the past, this process was a state responsibility and lacked consistency across Australia. It also required that if a teacher moved to another state or territory they had to apply for registration in that state or territory and often the process had different requirements and conditions.

Under the national process, state registration is transferable. New graduates are granted a provisional registration – or licence – to teach. They must work initially with a mentor teacher and have three years to demonstrate the proficient standard as set out in the Australian Professional Standards for Teachers and therefore acquire full registration to teach.

Nationally consistent rewards and recognition

In order to continue to encourage and lift the standards of the profession, AITSL has been given the task of developing a reward and recognition process. While at the time of writing this book the fine details are still being developed, the rewards will be provided to teachers who apply for and achieve the higher levels in the Australian Professional Standards for Teachers; namely, Highly Accomplished and Lead Teacher. Teachers have a role in developing the future of the profession and that requires continual improvement. In no other industry should the term 'lifelong learning' be more important to demonstrate than in education.

Nationally consistent performance and development processes

This is designed to improve teacher quality by providing a framework to assist schools to develop an effective performance and development process. This framework reflects national and international perspectives about what constitutes effective teacher development. While each school will decide how they develop their teachers, the framework serves as a guide and a reference point.

Australian Professional Standard for Principals

This standard sets out the complex work of the principal and is designed to guide professional learning and self-reflection. The nature of a principal's work is fluid, multifaceted, underpinned by the individual's set of values, knowledge and qualities, and cannot be represented simply by a hierarchy of skills. The standard aims to reflect the complexity of the role.

Australian Curriculum

The Australian Curriculum has defined what will be taught to students throughout the country at each year level in each learning area. Previously, this differed from state to state, although there were clear correlations. The Australian Curriculum makes it easier for teachers to know what has been taught to students who move between states and makes it easier for teachers who move interstate.

> *The introduction of a national curriculum makes the transition from various schools (through transfers) smoother and you can plan with a greater understanding of the prior learning as well as knowledge of where students will be going next (Christine Williams, primary, government)*

Early Years Learning Framework

This document establishes national standards, goals and expectations for the pre-school years of education. It describes appropriate curriculum and pedagogy for these years, and ensures that children in these years get the teaching and care they deserve.

> *What excites me the most at the moment is the introduction of the Early Years Learning Framework. This document considers the whole child and, based on research and wisdom. all early childhood teachers are encouraged to examine the importance of developmentally appropriate pedagogy and curriculum. (Kerrie van Abkoude, primary, government)*

International perspectives

This book is written primarily for an Australian audience. However, you may choose to teach in another country at some time in your life. Educators and education systems increasingly seek to learn from one another across international boundaries, so Australian education influences and is influenced by other countries. The directions for the future described here in Australia are consistent with trends throughout much of the world.

10

STARTING OUT[21]

I have been in the teaching profession for two years now and nothing you do at university could prepare you for the workplace. University courses prepare you with the foundations and theory behind teaching, but you will flourish in the practical setting, where all the theory comes to life and finally makes sense. (Melissa Hoppenbrouwers, primary, Catholic)

You've completed the training. You're qualified. You've been offered a job! You step into your new classroom. Suddenly, you discover what you *didn't* learn at university!

No training course can fully prepare you for the realities of life in the classroom. It's full-on, five days a week. There's the awesome responsibility of caring for students' safety, personal and social development and intellectual learning. Then there's the difficulty of dealing with parents who are much older than you. All your learning seems to go out the window when face to face with a parent who is concerned about their child. You rely on basic wisdom and self-confidence instead.

What is most salient to a teacher reflecting on their first year is how little they knew about teaching until they started. Although surrounded by kids, teaching is not a kids' world. You have adult responsibilities. Your work has to satisfy adult colleagues and adult parents.

Organisation

This involves learning to make decisions quickly, and accepting that you'll get some of them wrong. You have to do things once and then put them out of your mind, and to deal with matters immediately, not procrastinate.

Develop procedures for keeping tabs on what has to be done (the student who's leaving early, the report for the special education consultant, the feedback required on mathematics for the staff meeting, and a thousand other things). Scribbled notes on a hundred pieces of paper are useless, so an effective filing system is essential. Notes, resources, plans, permission slips, forms and budgets filed in a computer are a cinch to amend and re-use.

Get real

You have to be realistic about what you can do. There are so many new approaches and ideas to try and special events to arrange. They're all inviting, but there is neither preparation time nor time in class for them all. Focus instead on the important stuff and resist the temptation to spread too widely.

For example, you want to develop individually tailored programs, but it's difficult to spend the time you would like with each student. So you decide to group the class, in order to pitch lessons at each student's ability. But this means preparing three or four different lessons for each group! You quickly realise that you jus t have to work with larger groups of the whole class.

You also realise that the wonders of extension and remediation teaching are mostly a dream. Of course, you find ways to assist and stimulate individual students, but you may become frustrated by the time it takes.

Hitting the wall

Watch out for third term! At the start of the year, you power along on adrenalin — it's all new, exciting and challenging and there's enough happening to keep you going. You can set aside the few fits of depression as tiredness and frustration (and maybe homesickness) set in, but by third term (or thereabouts) you're way past the hype. You realise, with some dread, the inevitability of the morning alarm clock and the waiting faces.

Students learn to know your limits and precisely how to push you to them. Here 's where you really begin to tough it out! The procedures and routines you've set in place can, however, be relied upon to give you breathing space in which to plan strategies that deal with difficult students and to make learning more motivating. Also keep emphasising your expectations to students.

You could spend 25 hours a day, eight days a week, working at teaching, planning and following up what takes place in the classroom. And, at the end of such a week, you could still see more to do and achieve. Decide how much time to spend on the job and remember that you *do* have another life!

Doing things in the right order

Teaching is a complex task and you can't expect to excel at all aspects of it straight off. In the early months, what matters is your classroom management. Determine your expectations of students, discipline, procedures and routines, monitors and helpers, who goes where, when and how, class rules, what is and is not acceptable work — all the things that make the classroom function with a minimum of fuss.

You also need to find ways of coping with several things happening in the classroom at the same time. How can you handle several different groups – probably even different year levels – in the class? What do you do with the other students while you concentrate on the Year 3s? How do you prevent disruptions while occupied with another group?

Get to know your students. What type of lesson, topic or form of discipline does each respond to? Who causes trouble and who works well, and with whom? What can you expect from each student? And, don't forget, they are asking the same questions about you! What is likeable about this teacher? What gets them going? What can and can't I get away with? How? What are this teacher's expectations? Is this someone I would trust with my secrets? Will they look after me?

What to teach?

Initially, don't try to teach wildly creative material. Of course, it has to be relevant and appropriate, but pick topics you feel comfortable about teaching and can prepare with a minimum of hassle, or pick topics you've used on practicums.

When you have all the management strategies at hand and the routines and procedures in place (and that may take a while), you can start really thinking about what to teach and how. Try unfamiliar topics, grouping students differently, varying your teaching style – all those things you've seen, read or heard about that you think make for better teaching.

Birth of an educator

Over time, you will begin to recognise your preferred ways of working and classroom structures. You'll begin to respond to difficult students and situations almost without thinking. You'll anticipate problems and deal with them instinctively without trauma. Well, mostly. When a child throws up across a table of books for marking, you're entitled to be momentarily rattled!

Question your students' achievements. Are they doing as well as they might? Which learning methods seem to have the most impact? Are you catering for different abilities and different learning styles1 Are you achieving the goals you want for your students? Keep evaluating and change your approaches in the light of your experience or reading.

Of course, there's a limit to what you can do. Set yourself a goal each term, semester or year and work to achieve it. Find time to reflect on your teaching. Look for – and celebrate! – the ways that you make a difference to your students.

If, at the end of your first year, you know you've made a difference to your students and have been able to enjoy the other things that are important in your life, you've more than survived – you've succeeded. Now you're ready for all those ideas you put on hold until your second year.

First-timer priorities

Survive. Just get to the end of the day without losing it That's enough at first

Be realistic. Don't try to do more than you can cope with. It's better to do simple things well, than complex things badly.

Accept that teaching is a time-consuming occupation and that you will have work to do after hours, but maintain a balanced life, without guilt.

Learn to enjoy kids and teaching. Young people are fun to be with. If you relax and listen you will really enjoy them. (If you don't, find another job — quickly — for their sake and yours!) Teaching is rewarding. Learn to recognise the little gains that students make and to celebrate them.

Listen to the advice of others. Find someone who is experienced, positive about their job and their students and competent in their work. Talk to them and listen to them. Then try what they suggest. Don't ever see yourself as a liability; just accept that you have a lot to learn.

Laugh at your mistakes and embarrassments, even if you can't see the humour at the time. (I once looked up from what I was doing, noticed that the clock was on the hour and dismissed the kids to lunch. Their awkward smiles and glances suggested that things weren't right. I had dismissed them an hour early!)

What you lack in organisation and experience, you make up for in enthusiasm. Use this strength to carry you through problems where your experience is inadequate.

11

ONE TEACHER'S STORY

The dreams, hopes and possibilities for future generations of students are endless. (Susan Keith, Prep to Year 12, Catholic)

In this book we have suggested that teaching requires people who feel a calling or commitment to teaching and whose own schooling has been successful, as reflected in sound academic standards.

Yet there is a problem with this. Because most teachers are successful learners, many struggle to understand students who 'don't get it'. They assume that, if the material is presented clearly, sequenced appropriately and supported by examples and practice, then every student should understand it. Unfortunately, teaching is not always like this. And it is not necessarily the fault of the student. While teachers like to assume that a struggling student will succeed if they simply pay more attention, work harder or do more homework, that isn't the solution for some students. Our brains are all wired differently and some students simply do not understand some concepts.

Ironically, we consider it quite acceptable that some students are not able to learn music successfully, no matter how hard they practise; others will never make artists; still others will never excel at sport; and others struggle to understand science. Some will never learn to juggle or to solve cryptic crosswords. Yet we assume that every student can succeed — if they try hard enough — at reading, writing, spelling, mathematics and other school subjects which society identifies as essential to employment.

Sometimes, teachers who struggled as school students — academically, socially or emotionally — make excellent teachers, because they are able to relate to struggling students. Below is one such teacher's personal journey. This was written by Tracey Gray, co- author of this book.

Fire in the belly

I failed the school system. And I didn't slightly fail. I walked away with nothing but a strong sense that I had wasted 11 years of my life. I felt school was something you had to do and that only a small number of kids enjoyed it. I wasn't one of them.

I sat six exams in my final high school year and walked out of most of them after realising that I couldn't answer any of the questions. I knew the teachers didn't like me and the feeling was mutual. The parting comment from the headmistress was that I would amount to nothing. So I walked out of school and said goodbye to the institution that had not been interested in helping me be the best I could be.

So why at 42 years of age am I writing this now? This is not a sob story and I don't want sympathy. I was not an easy student by any means. However, my life held, and still holds, endless possibilities.

I am writing this for educators everywhere, especially those for whom schooling was a positive and successful experience, to provide a child's perspective on what school is like when they don't find it easy. This is designed to serve as inspiration to make school a wonderful experience for all children and create fires in their bellies for lifelong learning.

Educators have much power and influence, because many children spend more of their waking hours with teachers than anyone else. Teachers shape the next generation, including their thinking about education. Child psychologist Haim Ginott writes:

> I've come to a frightening conclusion that I am the decisive element in the classroom. It's my

> personal approach that creates the climate. It's my daily mood that makes the weather. As a teacher, I possess a tremendous power to make a child's life miserable or joyous. I can be a tool of torture or an instrument of inspiration. I can humiliate or heal. In all situations, it is my response that decides whether a crisis will be escalated or de-escalated and a child humanized or dehumanized.[22]

These should be the first words any pre-service teacher hears in order to understand the true implications of this enormous responsibility.

As an adult, I have wondered where my school experience went wrong. I wasn't from a broken family. My parents loved me and worked hard. Unfortunately, for me, many of my teachers were instruments of pain and my school experience was of embarrassment and feelings of inadequacy and failure.

I think I was six when I started school as we moved around Australia and England. I was perhaps a little late going to school and couldn't read and write — to the horror of my teacher. Primary school seemed quite a forbidding place and the teachers rarely smiled. Everyone was loud and seemed annoyed or grumpy. It was obvious why they were so grumpy: I had started school! I kept a very low profile and as teachers started yelling my profile shrank even more. I hid in cupboards throughout the day and periodically surfaced so that I wouldn't raise panic about my whereabouts. It was my survival strategy.

I moved to another school when I was about eight years old and I have only one memory of it: the daily reading to my teacher. I hated reading because I found it difficult. Although I would try to sound out the words, I would feel anxiety and panic. My teacher was kind at first, but as I became more nervous, she became more frustrated. Eventually, she slapped my legs for reading so poorly — these were the days when teachers were permitted to smack students — and I cried. Not surprisingly, the daily experience didn't tum my fear and dislike of reading around and I didn't get any better at it.

The following year I attended my next school. It was an old school with old-fashioned teachers who wore old-fashioned clothes, buttoned up to their chins. They were very strict and I don't remember any of them smiling at all. School gave me the sense that I wasn't good at anything. Some children were good at reading and writing, others were good at mathematics, yet others were brilliant at sport and swimming and some were popular, pretty, funny, loved by the teachers. And then there was me — not particularly popular and often the last chosen for teams, with the teacher saying, 'Someone has to choose her' — like I was a piece of rotten fruit.

So, school was hard work for me. Mathematics and English were my dreaded subjects. I would feel a sense of apprehension as the teacher asked for writing books to be opened ready for dictation, as it usually meant a ruler would be smacked against my hand for poor spelling and punctuation, scruffy writing and anything else that could be wrong. Surely, looking at what I had done right might have been a better strategy, as I had actually tried. Perhaps, then, I would have wanted to get a few more things right. Mathematics was a foreign language. The mathematics teacher was scary and I would never raise my hand in her class for fear of being turned to stone by a steely glare. When my name was called to answer a question I would freeze and hope that something useful would come out of my mouth – but it never did.

Then, the most wonderful teacher commenced at the school. Mr Smith smiled, never shouted and always acted as though he liked us. He played the guitar, sang and loved drama, and I started to enjoy school. Mr Smith was always there with a word of encouragement and a smile and he kindled my interest in drama and music. He encouraged me to audition for the school play, which he organised and directed. I worked really hard at the role I was allocated and I was pretty good. Just as things were looking up, I was faced with another challenge.

The school bully seemed to be drawn to me, even though I gave her a very wide berth. She often told me to meet her after school and said that if I didn't she would kill me. I was beaten up quite badly. Mum and Dad were very upset and spoke to the school, but to no avail. The school knew she was a bad girl, but what could they do? So most days I waited after school for my beating, terrified that she would actually kill me.

Around this time, my family moved to the Middle East. I couldn't adjust to the city school and failed the entrance exams for the British and American schools. However, the American school agreed to take me and run 'tests' to find out what was wrong with me. The tests that I had to endure included a hearing and eyesight test, IQ test, problem- olving test, association test, interpreting ink dot prints (probably to check if I was going to grow up to be a mass murderer, I thought) and the last test, which involved what I thought was a series of stupid questions, such as 'What would you do if your house was on fire?' I was feeling pretty insulted by this time, so when I was asked to build structures with blocks, I refused to do any more tests, yelled at the tester that I wasn't stupid and she could take her tests and shove them, and walked out.

However, the tests identified the problem: I was learning disabled! At 11 years of age, after being at four schools, the education system decided that I that I had an inability to learn. I had not responded to any school strategies so the problem was clearly me' I still had to go to school and attend lessons, but I had an 'inability to learn' so I wouldn't be expected to be able to do much at all. I remember leaving the meeting in which the school told my parents I couldn't learn, and thinking that it had finally been confirmed that I was stupid and I was going to grow up to do and be nothing. I felt pretty sad about that.

I stayed at the school for a further six months and then asked Mum and Dad if I could go to boarding school, as that might be better. The kids at boarding school in the stories I had heard seemed to have fun, so maybe I could too. Fortunately, my Dad's job allowed me to go to boarding school in the UK. So I began my boarding school life at 'the Nunnery on the Hill'.

Unfortunately, it was nothing like the books. My school records followed me to this school, so the teachers told me that they knew I was learning disabled. I was doomed from the start. I re ally tried hard to listen, write neatly, spell properly, be polite and prove them all wrong. My problem was that I loved to talk and ask 'Why1' I asked why in mathematics but was told 'because that is how the sum works'. I asked why in grammar and was told I was being insolent. I asked why in history and was sent out. I finally asked why in Latin and was not allowed to return to Latin classes.

I muddled through high school. I begged the mathematics teacher to give me extra help after class. She agreed, but allowed all her favourite students to join us too. I was then embarrassed to ask the questions in fear of sounding stupid, so only received superficial help and not what I needed. When my extra lessons were not proving to be any use she said that we were flogging a dead horse and should probably quit while we were ahead.

It was at this point that I totally gave up on education. I went through the motions of attending class, completing homework and superficially participating, but I had an inability to learn boring, irrelevant information presented by people who couldn't stand me. I worked really hard in drama and sat exam after exam and achieved well. The teacher was inspiring, fun and liked me — and thought I was really good at acting. In my final year I achieved my Bronze Medal in Dramatic Art from the London Academy of Music and Dramatic Art.

Having felt bad for such a long time, I was keen to do anything which made me feel good at school. For a child to endure six hours of failure, day in and day out, was the equivalent of being sent to prison. I didn't understand why teachers didn't like me, but I think they assumed I wasn't trying and that I was 'thick'. I returned the same feelings to them, as I was ashamed, embarrassed and assumed that there was something wrong with me. Yet something didn't add up. Mum and Dad didn't think there was anything wrong with me, yet all the experts at school were saying I was learning disabled. Who was right and who was wrong? I left school with my Bronze Medal in acting, a General Certificate of Secondary Education in religious education, a few friends — and the belief that I was stupid and couldn't learn.

I didn't know what to do next, as the thought of getting a job was out of the question; I couldn't go through more rejection and humiliation. So I enrolled in a secretarial college where I achieved well in all subjects. What was the difference? The content was relevant, as I needed these skills to get a job. My school records didn't follow me this time, and I didn't tell the college that I had an inability to learn, so the teachers had the same expectations of me as they had of other students.

I returned to Australia, as I was born here and felt that leaving England would be a positive thing to do. I gained a job at a building society as a clerk. During 10 years, I was promoted annually, until I was the head of training and development and managed the call centre. It was then I decided, with the encouragement of my husband, to enrol in a training and development degree at university. As I still didn't believe that I could achieve anything academically, I only signed up for the associate degree, thinking that it would be easier to get out of when I started to fail. I didn't fail. I did so well that I completed the full degree — and won an award for the highest achievement in the course. This was a real buzz, as it showed me that I could achieve anything that I put my mind to. I became the state advertising and training manager of a direct marketing company and enjoyed this new level of confidence in myself.

It was then that I had a nagging feeling that I should get into education and make a positive difference to children. So I applied for a Graduate Diploma in Education and was accepted. The program was tough. I had to conquer my anxiety of exams and the fear that I was stupid at school subjects. I had to unlearn a lot of misconceptions about mathematics, but my lecturers removed my fear. I achieved a high distinction. After teaching for a few years, I completed a master's degree.

I became a primary teacher, making a commitment that no child would ever hate school in my class. I love teaching. While I have empathy for my teachers, who felt huge frustration at my behaviour and inability to understand what they were trying to teach me, I also feel that it was their job to teach me and none had the right to dismiss me as a lost cause. I had lots of potential, but not many of them took the time to find what would engage me or light the fire in my belly.

I understand now that teachers generally love what they teach and are passionate about their content area – but teachers need to get their students excited about the subject too. Kids who ask 'Why?' are interested, but need more information, need to see the relevance of the lesson, how it relates to their experience and how it connects to the wider world. Facts don't inspire; stories do. Once you hook children into a story they are interested to learn the facts. Without a connection between student and teacher, minimal learning takes place. Children with whom you connect will walk on hot coals for you, because you inspire them and light the fire in their bellies.

Teaching students who struggle challenges teachers to explore new strategies until the child understands. When you see the spark of hope light up in their eyes it is the best job in the world. After ten years teaching adults and seven teaching children, I believe that learning is about relationships:

- human relationships – students want to do more and achieve more when they feel a strong relationship and a connection to the teacher and the lesson, and when what they are doing is engaging and inspiring
- personal relationships – students need to see the

connections between what they are doing and where that will take them

- local relationships — at the micro level, students need to understand how this learning can help them right now
- global relationships — at the macro level, students need to see how the learning connects to the bigger picture and makes a difference for them.

A few years ago, I heard Larry Brendtro, who works with at-risk youth, quote psychologist Urie Bronfenbrenner, who said, 'Everyone needs at least one adult who is irrationally crazy about him or her.'[23] My parents were like this, but I wanted my teachers, too, to be irrationally crazy about my learning and not give up on me. Educators must believe that everyone can learn. I have never met anyone who wanted his or her life to be a failure. Yet, unfortunately, I hear too many children, even at Year 3, say that they hate school. This breaks my heart, as their eyes are still full of wonder — and they have another nine years of school ahead of them. Will their hate for school be so deep that their self-belief and love of learning will disappear'.

So these are my messages to you, as you contemplate teaching as a career:

- You will have so much influence over young lives that it is frightening. Those children or teenagers are looking to you to have faith in them, to like them and to light the fire of learning in their bellies. If you can't make a positive difference to each child, you are in the wrong profession.

- Have empathy and compassion for children. Find the gift in every child.
- Effectiveness as a teacher does not simply equate to years of teaching. Constantly seek new ways to help your students succeed. Great teachers reflect on their craft and find new and better ways of engaging, teaching and demonstrating a love and joy of learning.
- School records are helpful, but be wary of dismissing students based on their past history. Be open to possibilities — you might be the one to make their eyes shine.
- Hear their stories; share yours. Stories connect and inspire; facts don't.
- Smile at all children! Say hello and make eye contact. If you need to be a grump to manage students, you are in the wrong profession.
- Never yell at students.
- Encourage your students to question. When they ask questions it may mean they are actually interested.
- Be a role model for thinking, questioning, learning, investigating and asking 'What if?' If the y know you will tell them the answer, then what is the point of them finding out?
- Show your love — of your work and your students.

difference to each child, you are in the wrong [illegible]

Have empathy and compassion for the [illegible] every child.

Effectiveness as a teacher does not simply [illegible] teaching. Constantly seek new ways to help your students succeed. Great teachers reflect on their craft [illegible] and how to make it engaging, facilitating [illegible] love and joy of learning.

School records are helpful, but [illegible] students based on their past behaviour [illegible] – you might be the one to [illegible]

[illegible]

CONCLUSION

So that is teaching. We have shared with you teachers' daily frustrations and their most noble goals; the impact of teaching on their bodies, minds and hearts; the realities teachers face and the aspirations teachers share.

It is wrong to suggest that teaching is unique — that teachers have stresses and difficulties and frustrations which are greater than or different from those of any other career or that teachers' work is noble beyond that of any other. We have not tried to create that impression. However, we have tried to point out the particular set of personal and professional qualities, the particular responsibilities and the particular mindset of a teacher.

If this book has struck a chord for you, then teaching may be a good fit for your future career. You will make an impact on the lives of thousands of children and young people and they will make an impact on yours.

> *Teaching is not a career; it is a way of life. It overwhelms you and enriches your soul at the same time. It is the most rewarding and exhausting job you could wish for and when it is in your blood it never leaves. (Tracie*

Heaton, primary, government)

APPENDIX 1: Australian University education courses

The authors cannot guarantee that this list is complete and up to date. Please check with the university. An online list of accredited courses for initial teacher education has been made available at

<http://www.aitsl.edu.au/reports/accredited-programs>.

Although the list below has been organised by state, several universities have campuses in other states and some have multiple campuses within the state. However, where a university has multiple campuses, each course may not be offered at each campus. A reliable and up-to-date profile of each university, including the locations of its campuses, can be found at

<http://www.universitiesaustralia.edu.au/page/217/australia-s-universities/university-profiles>

Courses may be available in full-time, part-time (on-site) or external mode. Please check with the university.

These courses have been chosen because they apply to the teaching of students in schools. There are related education courses not cited here. Doctoral courses are not included. Not all courses cited here provide entry-level qualifications for classroom teaching.

Many universities have bridging or university preparation courses for those who are not well prepared for the rigours of university study.

Australian Capital Territory

Australian Catholic University (Also in Victoria, Queensland, NSW)

Bachelor of Education – Early Childhood and Primary

Bachelor of Education – Primary

Bachelor of Teaching – Early Childhood

Graduate Certificate in Religious Education

Graduate Diploma of Education – Secondary

Graduate Diploma of Education – Secondary/Graduate Certificate in Religious Education

Graduate Diploma of Religious Education

Master of Education

Master of Education (By Research)

Master of Religious Education

Master of Teaching – Secondary

Master of Teaching – Secondary/Graduate

Postgraduate Certificate in Education

Australian National University

Bachelor of Asia-Pacific Studies/ Bachelor of Education – Secondary Teaching

Bachelor of Asia-Pacific Studies/ Graduate Diploma of Education

Bachelor of Commerce/ Graduate Diploma of Education

Bachelor of Economics/ Graduate Diploma of Education

Bachelor of Science/ Bachelor of Education – Secondary Teaching

University of Canberra (Also in Victoria)

Bachelor of Asia-Pacific Studies/ Bachelor of Education – Secondary Teaching

Bachelor of Education

Bachelor of Education (Graduate Entry)

Bachelor of Education – Early Childhood/Primary/ Secondary (Conversion)

Bachelor of Education – Secondary Music

Bachelor of Education/ Bachelor of Arts

Bachelor of Education/ Bachelor of Science

Bachelor of Science/ Bachelor of Education – Secondary Teaching

Bachelor of Teaching (Graduate Entry)

Graduate Certificate in Education

Graduate Certificate in Scaffolding English for Speakers of Other Languages

Graduate Certificate in Teaching English to Speakers of Other Languages (TESOL) and Foreign Language Teaching

Graduate Diploma of Education – Secondary

Graduate Diploma of Teaching English to Speakers of Other Languages (TESOL) and Foreign Language Teaching

Master of Arts – Teaching English to Speakers of Other Languages (TESOL) and Foreign Language Teaching

Master of Community and Educational Leadership

Master of Education

Master of Education (By Research)

Master of Educational Leadership

New South Wales

Avondale College of Higher Education

Bachelor of Arts/ Bachelor of Teaching

Bachelor of Business/ Bachelor of Teaching

Bachelor of Education – Early Childhood

Bachelor of Education – Primary

Bachelor of Education – Secondary

Bachelor of Science/ Bachelor of Teaching

Bachelor of Teaching – Primary (Graduate Entry)

Bachelor of Teaching – Secondary (Graduate Entry)

Master of Education

Master of Education (By Research)

Australian College of Physical Education

Bachelor of Dance Education

Graduate Diploma of Education

Charles Sturt University (CSU)

Bachelor of Arts/Bachelor of Teaching – Secondary

Bachelor of Education – Birth to Five Years

Bachelor of Education – Early Childhood and Primary

Bachelor of Education – Health and Physical Education

Bachelor of Education – K-12 Middle Schooling

Bachelor of Education – Primary

Bachelor of Education – Secondary Mathematics – Industry Entry

Bachelor of Education – Technology and Applied Studies

Bachelor of Educational Studies

Bachelor of Teaching – Primary (Graduate Entry)

Bachelor of Teaching – Secondary (Graduate Entry)

Graduate Certificate in Classroom Technology

Graduate Certificate in Educational Research

Graduate Certificate in Inclusive Education

Graduate Certificate in Indigenous Education

Graduate Certificate in Learning and Teaching – Higher Education

Graduate Certificate in Literacy

Graduate Certificate in Literacy and Numeracy – Early Years

Graduate Certificate in Religious and Values Education

Graduate Certificate in Secondary Education

Graduate Certificate in TESOL

Graduate Diploma of Inclusive Education

Graduate Diploma of Vocational

Education and Training Master of Education

Master of Education – Teacher Librarianship

Master of Inclusive Education

Master of Information and Communication Technology in Education

Master of TESOL – Teaching English to Speakers of Other Languages

Macquarie University (Also in Victoria)

Bachelor of Arts

Bachelor of Arts – Psychology/Diploma of Education

Bachelor of Arts/Bachelor of Commerce

Bachelor of Arts/Bachelor of Education – Primary

Bachelor of Arts/Bachelor of Science

Bachelor of Arts/Diploma in Education

Bachelor of Education – Early Childhood

Education – Birth to 12

Bachelor of Education – Primary (Graduate Entry)

Bachelor of Science/Diploma of Education

Bachelor of Teaching – Birth to Five Years

Graduate Diploma of Early Childhood (Advanced)

Graduate Diploma of Early Childhood Teaching

Graduate Diploma of Education – Secondary

Master of Early Childhood

Master of Education

Master of Educational Leadership

Master of Environmental Education

Master of Indigenous Education

Master of Special Education

Master of Teaching – Birth to Five Years

Postgraduate Certificate in Early Childhood

Postgraduate Certificate in Education Studies

Postgraduate Certificate in Educational Leadership – Early Childhood Education

Postgraduate Certificate in Environmental Education

Postgraduate Certificate in Indigenous Education

Postgraduate Certificate in Special Education

Postgraduate Certificate in TESOL

Postgraduate Diploma of Early Childhood

Postgraduate Diploma of Education Studies

Postgraduate Diploma of Educational Leadership

Postgraduate Diploma of Environmental Education

Postgraduate Diploma of Indigenous Education

Postgraduate Diploma of Special Education

Morling College

Graduate Diploma of Education

Graduate Diploma of Education – Secondary

Master of Education

Master of Education – Leadership

Southern Cross University {SCU)

Bachelor of Arts/Bachelor of Education – Secondary

Bachelor of Contemporary Music/Bachelor of Education – Secondary

Bachelor of Education – Early Childhood

Bachelor of Education – Primary

Bachelor of Education – Secondary (Graduate Entry)

Bachelor of Science/Bachelor of Education – Secondary

Bachelor of Sport and Exercise Science/ Bachelor of Education – Secondary

Bachelor of Teaching – Primary (Graduate Entry)

Bachelor of Technology Education

Bachelor of Visual Arts/Bachelor of Education – Secondary

Graduate Diploma of Education – Secondary

Graduate Diploma of Vocational Education and Training

Master of Education

Master of Vocational Education and Training

University of New England

Advanced Diploma of Special Education and Disability Studies

Bachelor of Arts/Bachelor of Teaching

Bachelor of Business/Bachelor of Teaching

Bachelor of Education – Early Childhood (Graduate Entry)

Bachelor of Education – Early Childhood and Primary

Bachelor of Education – K-12 Teaching

Bachelor of Education – Primary

Bachelor of Information Technology/ Bachelor of Teaching

Bachelor of Mathematics/ Bachelor of Teaching

Bachelor of Music/ Bachelor of Teaching

Bachelor of Science/ Bachelor of Teaching

Bachelor of Special Education – Primary/ Bachelor of Disability Studies

Bachelor of Teaching – Early Childhood Education

Graduate Certificate in E-Learning

Graduate Certificate in Education Studies

Graduate Certificate in Gifted and Talented Education

Graduate Certificate in History Curriculum

Graduate Certificate in Indigenous Australian Education

Graduate Certificate in School Leadership

Graduate Certificate in Special Education

Graduate Certificate in Teaching English to Speakers of Other Languages (TESOL)

Graduate Diploma of Education

Master of Education

Master of Education (By Research)

Master of Teaching – Primary

Master of Teaching – Secondary

University of NSW

Bachelor of Art Education

Bachelor of Art Theory/Bachelor of Arts

Bachelor of Arts/Bachelor of Education – Secondary

Bachelor of Commerce/Bachelor of Education – Secondary

Bachelor of Design/Bachelor of Art Education

Bachelor of Economics/Bachelor of Education – Secondary

Bachelor of Fine Arts/Bachelor of Arts

Bachelor of Music/Bachelor of Education

Bachelor of Science – Computer Science/Bachelor of Arts

Bachelor of Science/Bachelor of Education

Graduate Certificate in Arts – TESOL

Graduate Certificate 1n Education

Graduate Certificate in Educational Leadership

Graduate Diploma of Arts – TESOL

Graduate Diploma of Education – Secondary

Master of Art and Design Education Master of Education

Master of Education (By Research)

Master of Educational Leadership

Master of Educational Leadership (By Research)

Master of Music Education (By Research)

Master of Teaching – Secondary

University of Newcastle

Master of Early Childhood Education

Master of Educational Studies

Master of Leadership and Management in Education

Master of Special Education

Master of Teaching – Primary

Master of Teaching – Secondary

University of Sydney

Bachelor of Education – Early Childhood

Bachelor of Education – Primary

Bachelor of Education – Secondary Human Movement and Health Education

Bachelor of Education – Secondary Humanities and Social Sciences/ Bachelor of Arts

Bachelor of Education – Secondary Mathematics/Bachelor of Science

Bachelor of Education – Secondary Science/Bachelor of Science

Bachelor of Music – Music Education

Bachelor of Music Studies/Bachelor of Arts

Bachelor of Teaching/Master of Teaching (Graduate Entry)

Graduate Certificate in Educational Studies

Graduate Certificate in Learning Science and Technology

Graduate Certificate in Teaching English as a Foreign Language

Graduate Diploma of Educational Studies

Graduate Diploma of Indigenous Languages Education

Graduate Diploma of Learning Science and Technology

Master of Education

Master of Education (By Research)

Master of Indigenous Languages Education

Master of Learning Science and Technology

Master of Music – Music Education (By Research)

Master of Philosophy – Education (By Research)

Master of Teaching

University of Technology, Sydney {UTS)

Bachelor of Education – Primary Education

Bachelor of Education/Bachelor of Arts – International Studies

Bachelor of Teaching – Secondary Education (Graduate Entry)

Graduate Certificate in Teaching English to Speakers of Other Languages

Graduate Diploma of Teaching English to Speakers of Other Languages (TESOL)

Master of Arts

Master of Arts – Teaching English to Speakers of Other Languages

Master of Education

Master of Education (By Research)

University of Western Sydney (UWS)

Bachelor of Arts/Master of Teaching – Primary

Bachelor of Arts/Master of Teaching – Secondary

Bachelor of Education – Birth-5 Years

Bachelor of Education – Primary AREP

Bachelor of Science/Master of Teaching – Secondary

Bachelor of Social Science/Master of Teaching – Birth-5 Years/Birth-12 Years

Graduate Certificate in Education – Social Ecology

Graduate Certificate in Special Education Studies

Graduate Certificate in TESOL

Graduate Diploma of TESOL

Master of Arts – TESOL

Master of Education – Leadership

Master of Education – Social Ecology

Master of Special Education

Master of Teaching – Birth-5 Years/ Birth-12 Years

Master of Teaching – Primary

Master of Teaching – Secondary

University of Wollongong (UOW)

Bachelor of Education – The Early Years

Bachelor of Mathematics Education

Bachelor of Physical and Health Education

Bachelor of Primary Education

Bachelor of Science Education

Graduate Certificate in Computer Based Learning

Graduate Certificate in Early Years Education

Graduate Certificate in Educational Leadership

Graduate Certificate in Gifted Education

Graduate Certificate in Literacy Leadership

Graduate Certificate in Physical and Health Education

Graduate Certificate in Special Education

Graduate Certificate in Teaching English to Speakers of Other Languages (TESOL)

Graduate Diploma of Education – Primary

Graduate Diploma of Education – Secondary

Graduate Diploma of Teaching English to Speakers of Other Languages (TESOL)

Master of Arts – Education (By Research)

Master of Education

Master of Education (By Research)

Master of Education – Interdisciplinary

Studies in Education

Master of Physical and Health Education

Wesley Institute

Graduate Diploma of Education – Secondary

Master of Teaching – Primary

Alphacrucis College Ltd (Also Queensland, Victoria)

Master of Teaching – Primary

Northern Territory

Batchelor Institute of Indigenous Tertiary Education

Bachelor of Education – Primary Teaching

Bachelor of Teaching and Learning – Early Childhood

Charles Darwin University (CDU)

Bachelor of Early Childhood Learning

Bachelor of Education – Primary Teaching

Bachelor of Education – Secondary Teaching

Bachelor of Teaching and Learning – Early Childhood

Bachelor of Teaching and Learning – Early Childhood (lnservice)

Graduate Certificate in Indigenous Education

Graduate Diploma of Language Teaching

Graduate Diploma of Teaching and Learning

Master of Education

Queensland

Bond University

Graduate Certificate in TESOL

Master of Arts – TESOL/LOTE

Central Queensland University (CQU)

Bachelor of Learning Design

Bachelor of Learning Management – Early Childhood Education

Bachelor of Learning Management – Primary Education

Bachelor of Learning Management – Secondary and Vocational Education and Training

Graduate Certificate in E-Learning

Graduate Certificate in Learning

Management – Specialisation

Graduate Diploma of E-Learning

Graduate Diploma of Learning and Teaching – Specialisation

Master of Learning Management – Specialisation

Christian Heritage College

Bachelor of Arts/Bachelor of Education – Secondary

Bachelor of Education – Middle Years

Bachelor of Education – Primary

Bachelor of Education – Secondary

Graduate Certificate in Christian Education

Graduate Diploma of Education – Primary

Graduate Diploma of Education – Secondary

Master of Education

Griffith University

Bachelor of Child and Family Studies/ Bachelor of Education – Primary

Bachelor of Education – Primary

Bachelor of Education – Secondary

Bachelor of Education – Special Education

Graduate Certificate in Autism Studies

Graduate Certificate in Drama Education

Graduate Certificate in Education Studies

Graduate Certificate in Educational Leadership

Graduate Certificate in Science – Science Education

Graduate Certificate in Special Education

Graduate Certificate in Teaching English to Speakers of Other Languages (TESOL)

Graduate Diploma of Early Childhood Education

Graduate Diploma of Education – Primary

Graduate Diploma of Education – Secondary

Master of Applied Theatre and Drama Education

Master of Arts – Applied Linguistics/ Teaching English to

Speakers of Other Languages
Master of Autism Studies
Master of Early Childhood Education
Master of Education
Master of Science – Science Education
Master of Special Education
Master of Teaching – Primary
Master of Teaching – Professional Practice – Primary
Master of Teaching – Professional Practice – Secondary
Master of Teaching – Secondary

James Cook University (JCU)

Bachelor of Education
Bachelor of Education – Professional Development (Graduate Entry)
Bachelor of Education – RATEP
Bachelor of Education/Bachelor of Arts
Bachelor of Education/Bachelor of Languages
Bachelor of Education/Bachelor of Science
Bachelor of Sports and Exercise Science/ Bachelor of Education
Graduate Certificate in Catholic Education
Graduate Certificate in Education for Sustainability
Graduate Diploma of Education
Master of Education
Postgraduate Certificate in Education

Queensland University of Technology (QUT)

Bachelor of Early Childhood

Bachelor of Early Childhood Studies

Bachelor of Education – Early Childhood

Bachelor of Education – Pre-service Early Childhood

Bachelor of Education – Primary Bachelor of Education – Secondary

Bachelor of Education – Secondary – Home Economics

Bachelor of Education – Secondary – Physical Education

Bachelor of Exercise and Movement Science/Bachelor of Education – Secondary

Graduate Certificate in Education

Graduate Diploma of Education

Master of Education

Master of Education (By Research)

University of Queensland {UQ)

Bachelor of Arts/Bachelor of Education – Secondary

Bachelor of Business Management

Bachelor of Education – Secondary

Bachelor of Creative Arts/Bachelor of Education – Secondary

Bachelor of Education – Middle Years of Schooling

Bachelor of Education – Primary

Bachelor of Health, Sport and Physical Education

Bachelor of Music/Bachelor of Education – Secondary

Bachelor of Science/Bachelor of Education – Secondary
Graduate Certificate in Applied Linguistics

Graduate Certificate in Educational Studies

Graduate Diploma of Applied Linguistics

Graduate Diploma of Education

Graduate Diploma of Educational Studies

Master of Applied Linguistics

Master of Applied Linguistics (Advanced)

Master of Educational Studies

Master of Educational Studies (Advanced)

University of Southern Queensland {USQ)

Bachelor of Early Childhood

Bachelor of Education – Early Childhood

Bachelor of Education – Primary

Bachelor of Education – Secondary Bachelor of Education – Special Education

Bachelor of Education – Sport, Health and Physical Education – Primary

Bachelor of Education – Sport, Health and Physical Education – Secondary

Graduate Diploma of Learning and Teaching

Graduate Diploma of Teaching

Master of Education

Master of Learning and Development
Master of Professional Studies
Postgraduate Certificate in Education
Postgraduate Certificate in Learning and Development

University of the Sunshine Coast (USC)

Bachelor of Early Childhood Education
Bachelor of Education
Bachelor of Education/Bachelor of Arts Bachelor of Education/Bachelor of Business
Bachelor of Education/Bachelor of Science
Bachelor of Primary Education
Graduate Certificate in Professional Learning
Graduate Diploma of Education – Preparatory to Year Three
Graduate Diploma of Education – Primary
Graduate Diploma of Education – Secondary
Master of Education
Master of Education (By Research)
Master of TESOL Education

South Australia

Flinders University

Bachelor of Education – Early Childhood/Bachelor of Arts

Bachelor of Education – Early Childhood and Special Education/Bachelor of Disability Stu dies

Bachelor of Education – Middle and Secondary and Special Education/ Bachelor of Disability Studies

Bachelor of Education – Middle and Secondary Schooling/Bachelor of Arts

Bachelor of Education – Middle and Secondary Schooling/Bachelor of Health Sciences

Bachelor of Education – Middle and Secondary Schooling/Bachelor of Science

Bachelor of Education – Primary R-7/ Bachelor of Arts

Bachelor of Education – Primary R-7 and Special Education/Bachelor of Disability Studies

Bachelor of Education – Secondary Schooling/Bachelor of Languages

Bachelor of Special Education (Graduate Entry)

Graduate Certificate in Education

Graduate Certificate in Education – Behaviour

Graduate Certificate in Education – Cognitive Psychology and Educational Practice

Graduate Certificate in Education – Gifted Education

Graduate Certificate in Education – Higher Education

Graduate Certificate in Education – International Baccalaureate Middle Years Program

Graduate Certificate in Education – Leadership and Management

Graduate Certificate in Education– Learning Difficulties

Graduate Certificate in Education – Professional Learning

Graduate Certificate in Education – Special Education

Graduate Certificate in Education – Studies of Asia

Graduate Certificate in Education – Vision Impairment

Graduate Certificate in Education – Vocational Education and Training in Schools

Grad u ate Certificate in Language Teaching

Graduate Certificate in Teaching English as a Second Language

Graduate Diploma of Language Teaching

Graduate Diploma of Teaching English as a Second Language

Master of Arts – Teaching English as a Second Language

Master of Education

Master of Education – Educational Research Evaluation and Assessment

Master of Education – Gifted Education

Master of Education – International Baccalaureate

Master of Education – Leadership and Management

Master of Education – Special Education

Master of Education – Studies of Asia

Master of Teaching – Early Childhood

Master of Teaching – Primary R-7

Master of Teaching – Secondary

Master of Teaching – Special Education Primary R-7

Master of Teaching – Special Education Secondary

Master of Teaching English as a Second Language

Tabor Adelaide

Bachelor of Arts and Education – Secondary

Bachelor of Education – Middle School

Bachelor of Education – Middle School (Graduate Entry)

Bachelor of Education – Primary

Bachelor of Education – Primary (Graduate Entry)

Bachelor of Education – Secondary (Graduate Entry)

Master of Education

University of Adelaide

Bachelor of Teaching/Bachelor of Arts

Bachelor of Teaching/Bachelor of Economics

Bachelor of Teaching/Bachelor of Mathematics and Computer Science

Bachelor of Teaching/Bachelor of Science

Graduate Certificate in Education

Graduate Diploma of Education

Graduate Diploma of Educational Studies

Master of Education

Postgraduate Certificate in Education

University of South Australia

Bachelor of Arts – Aboriginal Studies/Bachelor of Education – Middle and Secondary

Bachelor of Arts – Australian Studies/ Bachelor of Education – Middle and Secondary

Bachelor of Early Childhood Education (Inservice)

Bachelor of Education – Design and Technology Education

Bachelor of Education – Early Childhood

Bachelor of Education – Primary

Bachelor of Education – Primary and Middle

Bachelor of Science/Bachelor of Education

Graduate Certificate in Education

Graduate Certificate in Education – Academic Practice

Graduate Certificate in Education – Catholic Education

Graduate Certificate in Education – Early Childhood Leadership

Graduate Certificate in Education – Educational Leadership and Management

Graduate Certificate in Education – Teaching English to Speakers of Other Languages

Graduate Diploma of Education – Secondary

Master of Catholic Education

Master of Education

Master of Teaching – Early Childhood

Master of Teaching – Junior Primary and Primary

Master of Teaching – Middle and Secondary

Master of Teaching – Primary and Middle

Tasmania

University of Tasmania

Bachelor of Education

Bachelor of Education – Applied Learning

Bachelor of Education – Early Childhood

Bachelor of Education – Primary

Graduate Certificate in Education

Graduate Certificate in Science Education

Master of Education

Master of Education (By Research)

Master of Teaching

Victoria

Deakin University

Bachelor of Early Childhood Education

Bachelor of Education – Primary

Bachelor of Health and Physical Education

Bachelor of Teaching – Science/Bachelor of Science

Bachelor of Teaching – Secondary/ Bachelor of Arts

Graduate Certificate in Education – Teaching English to Speakers of Other Languages (TESOL)

Graduate Diploma of Teaching – Primary

Master of Arts – Education (By Research)

Master of Education

Master of Education – Educational Leadership and Administration

Master of Education – Special Educational Needs

Master of Education – Teaching English to Speakers of Other Languages (TESOL)

Master of Education – Teaching Languages Other than English (LOTE)

Master of Teaching

Master of Teaching English to Speakers of Other Languages

La Trobe University

Bachelor of Arts/ Bachelor of Arts Education

Bachelor of Early Childhood Education

Bachelor of Education

Bachelor of Outdoor Education

Bachelor of Outdoor Environmental Education

Bachelor of Outdoor Recreation Education

Bachelor of Physical and Health Education

Bachelor of Physical and Outdoor Education

Bachelor of Science/Bachelor of Science Education

Bachelor of Teaching – Primary

Bachelor of Teaching – Secondary

Graduate Certificate in Education – Teaching English to

Speakers of Other Languages (TESOL)

Graduate Certificate in Outdoor and Environmental Education

Graduate Certificate in Special Education and Human Services

Graduate Diploma of Education – Middle Years

Graduate Diploma of Education – Primary

Graduate Diploma of Education – Secondary

Graduate Diploma of Educational Studies

Graduate Diploma of Outdoor and Environmental Education

Graduate Diploma of Technology Education

Graduate Diploma of TESOL

Master of Education

Master of Education (By Research)

Master of Educational Leadership and Management

Master of Outdoor and Environmental Education

Master of Special Education

Master of Teaching – P-12 Master of TESOL

Melbourne Institute of Technology (MIT)

Bachelor of Education

Monash University

Bachelor of Arts/Bachelor of Education – Primary

Bachelor of Arts/Bachelor of Education – Secondary

Bachelor of Arts and Social Sciences/ Bachelor of Education – Primary

Bachelor of Commerce/Bachelor of Education – Secondary

Bachelor of Early Childhood Education

Bachelor of Early Childhood Studies

Bachelor of Education – P-10

Bachelor of Education – Special Education

Bachelor of Mu sic/Bachelor of Education – Primary

Bachelor of Mu sic/Bachelor of Education – Secondary

Bachelor of Primary Education

Bachelor of Science/Bachelor of Education – Primary

Bachelor of Science/Bachelor of Education – Secondary

Bachelor of Sport and Outdoor Recreation/Bachelor of Education – Primary

Bachelor of Sport and Outdoor Recreation/Bachelor of Education – Secondary

Bachelor of Visual Arts/Bachelor of Education – Primary

Bachelor of Visual Arts/Bachelor of Education – Secondary

Graduate Diploma of Mental Health for Teaching Professions

Master of Applied Linguistics for Language Teachers

Master of Education

Master of Education (By Coursework and Research)

Master of Education (By Research)

Master of Education – Teaching English to Speakers of Other Languages (TESOL) – International

Master of School Leadership

Master of Teaching – Early Childhood

Master of Teaching – Primary

Master of Teaching – Secondary

Post graduate Diploma of Education

Open Universities Australia (OUA)

Bachelor of Education – Early Childhood Education

Bachelor of Education – Primary

Graduate Certificate in E-Learning

Graduate Certificate in Education Law

Graduate Certificate in Middle Years Education

Graduate Certificate in Teaching English to Speakers of Other Languages (TESOL)

Graduate Certificate in Tertiary Teaching

Graduate Diploma of Education – Primary

Graduate Diploma of Education – Secondary

Master of Science – Science and Mathematics Education

RMIT University

Bachelor of Applied Science – Physical Education

Bachelor of Education (Graduate Entry)

Bachelor of Education (Primary and Arts Expertise)

Bachelor of Education – Early Childhood Education

Bachelor of Education/Bachelor of Applied Science – Disability

Graduate Certificate in Careers Education and Development

Graduate Certificate in Educational Leadership and Management

Graduate Diploma of Careers Education and Development
Graduate Diploma of Early Childhood Teaching
Graduate Diploma of Education – Early Childhood
Graduate Diploma of Education – Primary
Graduate Diploma of Education – Secondary
Graduate Diploma of Educational Leadership and Management
Master of Arts – Education (By Research)
Master of Education
Master of Education (By Research)

Tabor College (Victoria) Inc

Graduate Diploma of Education – Primary

University of Ballarat

Bachelor of Education
Bachelor of Education – Early Childhood
Bachelor of Education – Physical Education
Bachelor of Mathematical Sciences/ Bachelor of Education
Bachelor of Science/Bachelor of Education
Bachelor of Teaching – Early Childhood Education
Bachelor of Visual Arts/Bachelor of Education
Graduate Certificate in Outdoor and Environmental Education
Graduate Diploma of Education – Primary
Graduate Diploma of Education – Secondary
Graduate Diploma of Outdoor and Environmental Education

Master of Education (By Research)

Master of Education Studies

Master of Special Education

Postgraduate Diploma of Education Studies – Early Childhood

University of Melbourne

Master of Education

Master of Education – Educational Management

Master of Education – International Baccalaureate (By Research)

Master of Education – Language Intervention and Hearing Impairment

Master of Education – Special Education, Inclusion and Early Intervention

Master of Education – Specific Learning Difficulties

Master of Education – Student Wellbeing

Master of Education Policy – International

Master of Educational Psychology Master of Evaluation

Master of Modern Languages Education

Master of Music – Performance Teaching

Master of Music Studies (Intensive)

Master of Teaching – Early Childhood

Master of Teaching – Primary

Master of Teaching – Secondary

Master of Teaching English to Speakers of Other Languages (TESOL)

Postgraduate Certificate in Education

Postgraduate Certificate in Education – International Baccalaureate

Postgraduate Certificate in Education – Language Intervention and Hearing Impairment

Postgraduate Certificate in Education – Special Education, Inclusion and Early Intervention

Postgraduate Certificate in Education – Specific Learning Difficulties

Po st graduate Certificate in Educational Research

Postgraduate Certificate in Modern Languages Education

Postgraduate Certificate in Teaching English to Speakers of Other Languages (TESOL)

Victoria University {VU}

Bachelor of Applied Science – Physical Education – Secondary

Bachelor of Education – Early Childhood/Primary

Bachelor of Education – Early Childhood/Primary (Accelerated)

Bachelor of Education – Prep-Year 12

Bachelor of Education – Prep-Year 12 (Accelerated)

Graduate Certificate in Teaching English to Speakers of Other Languages (TESOL)

Graduate Diploma of Early Childhood Education

Graduate Diploma of Early Childhood Teaching

Graduate Diploma of Educational Learning and Leadership

Graduate Diploma of Primary Teaching

Graduate Diploma of Secondary Education

Graduate Diploma of Teaching English to Speakers of Other Languages (TESOL)

Master of Education

Master of Education (By Research)

Master of Education – VET

Master of Teaching

Master of Teaching English to Speakers of Other Languages (TESOL)

Western Australia

Curtin University

Bachelor of Arts – Early Education

Bachelor of Education – Early Childhood Education

Bachelor of Education – Primary Education

Bachelor of Education – Secondary Education

Graduate Certificate in Teaching English to Speakers of Other Languages (TESOL)

Graduate Diploma of Education – Secondary Education

Master of Education

Master of Philosophy – Education (By Research)

Master of Philosophy– Mathematics Education (By Research)

Master of Philosophy – Science Education (By Research)

Master of Science – Science and Mathematics Education

Edith Cowan University (ECU)

Bachelor of Education – Early Childhood Studies

Bachelor of Education – Primary

Bachelor of Education – Secondary

Graduate Certificate in Behaviour Management

Graduate Certificate in Education – Early Childhood Studies

Graduate Certificate in Education – Educational Leadership

Graduate Certificate in Education – Learning Difficulties

Graduate Certificate in Education – Literacy Education

Graduate Certificate 1n Education – Special Education

Graduate Certificate in Education – Teaching English to Speakers of Other Languages (TESOL)

Graduate Diploma of Education – Early Childhood Studies

Graduate Diploma of Education – Primary

Graduate Diploma of Education – Secondary

Master of Career Development

Master of Education

Master of Education (By Research)

Murdoch University

Bachelor of Education – Early Childhood and Primary Teaching

Bachelor of Education – Primary

Bachelor of Education – Primary (Graduate Entry)

Bachelor of Education – Primary/ Bachelor of Arts – Australian Indigenous Studies

Bachelor of Education – Primary, 1-10 Health and Physical Education

Bachelor of Education – Secondary (Combined Degree)

Bachelor of Education – Secondary (Graduate Entry)

Bachelor of Education – Secondary/ Bachelor of Arts

Bachelor of Education – Secondary/ Bachelor of Arts – Theatre and Drama

Bachelor of Education – Secondary/ Bachelor of Science

Bachelor of Education – Secondary/ Bachelor of Sports Science

Graduate Certificate in Drama Teaching

Graduate Certificate in Early Childhood Education

Graduate Certificate in Education Studies

Graduate Certificate in Inclusive Education

Graduate Certificate in Mathematics Teaching

Graduate Diploma of Education – Primary

Graduate Diploma of Education – Secondary

Graduate Diploma of Education Studies

Master of Education

Master of Education (By Research)

Postgraduate Certificate in Gifted and Talented Education

University of Notre Dame Australia (Also in NSW)

Bachelor of Arts/Graduate Diploma of Education – Secondary

Bachelor of Education – Early Childhood and Care: 0-8 Years

Bachelor of Education – Early Childhood and Care: 0-8

Years/Bachelor of Arts

Bachelor of Education – Early Childhood

and Care: 0-8 Years/Bachelor of Behavioural Science

Bachelor of Education – Early Childhood and Care: 0-8 Years/Bachelor of Science

Bachelor of Education – Kindergarten to Year 7

Bachelor of Education – Primary

Bachelor of Education – Primary/Bachelor of Arts

Bachelor of Education – Primary/Bachelor of Behavioural Science

Bachelor of Education – Primary/Bachelor of Science

Bachelor of Education – Secondary

Bachelor of Education – Secondary/

Bachelor of Arts

Bachelor of Education – Secondary/Bachelor of Behavioural Science

Bachelor of Education – Secondary/

Bachelor of Science Bachelor of Health and Physical Education – Primary

Bachelor of Health and Physical Education – Secondary

Bachelor of Science/Graduate Diploma of Education – Secondary

Graduate Certificate in Education Graduate Certificate in Religious Education

Graduate Diploma of Education – Secondary

Graduate Diploma of Outdoor Education

Master of Education

Master of Education (By Research)

Master of Outdoor Education

Master of Teaching – Primary

Master of Teaching – Secondary

University of Western Australia (UWA}

Graduate Diploma of Education

Graduate Diploma of Educational Studies

Graduate Diploma of Professional Education

Master of Education

Master of Education (By Research)

Master of Education (By Thesis and Coursework)

Master of Education Research Methods

Master of Science Communication and Education

Master of Science Education (By Research)

Master of Teaching

REFERENCES

[1] J Hattie, *Teachers make a difference: What is the research evidence?*, Australian Council for Educational Research, Melbourne, 2003.

[2] P McKenzie, G Rowley, P Weldon & M Murphy, *Staff in Australia's schools 2010: Main report on the survey,* Australian Council for Educational Research and Australian Government Department of Education, Employment and Workplace Relations, Melbourne, 2011, p. 48.

[3] CF Mansfield, AE Price, S Beltman, A Mcconney, LC Pelliccione & M Wosnitza, *Keeping cool: Embedding resilience in the initial teacher education curriculum: Final report,* Office of Learning and Teaching, Sydney, p. 3.

[4] P Ridden, *For those who teach,* Australian Council for Educational Research, Melbourne, 2012, pp. 93-94.

[5] B Jensen & J Reichl, Better *teacher appraisal and feedback: Improving performance,* Grattan Institute, Melbourne, 2011.

[6] La Trobe University, 'Qualities of a good teacher', Melbourne, 2013, <http://www.latrobe.edu.au/education/becoming-a-teacher/qualities>, accessed 15 March 2013.

---

[7] Queensland Government Department of Education, 'Training and Employment, 'Qualities of a good teacher', Brisbane, 2012, <http://education.qld.gov.au/hr/recruitment/Teaching/qualities-good-teacher. html>, accessed 15 March 2013.

[8] E Jean Khawajkie, A Muller, S Niedemayer, U Jolis & C Jolis, *What makes a good teacher?* Children *speak their minds,* International Consultative Forum on Education for All, UNESCO, Paris, 1996, unpaged, <http://unesdoc.unesco.org/images/0010/001041/104124m.pdf>, accessed 15 March 2013.

[9] Mansfield et al, op. cit., pp. 14-15.

[10] Commonwealth of Australia, 'Higher standards for teacher training courses', Canberra, 2013, <http://www.betterschools.gov.au/docs/higher-standards-teacher-training-courses>, accessed 23 March 2013.

[11] J Tovey & A McNeilage, 'The new Rs needed for teaching: reading, writing and a bucketload of rapport ', *National Times,* 11 March 2013, <http://www.national times.com.au/opinion/political-news/the-new-rs-needed-for-teaching-reading-writing-and-a-bucketload-of-rapport-20130311-2fwg7.html?rand=1363029705448>, accessed 23 March 2013.

[12] P Medlen, 'The crowded curriculum', ABC News Online, 22 June 2010, <http://abc.net.au/news/2010-06-22/the-crowded-curriculum/876076>, accessed 15 March 2013.

[13] N Dulfer, S Rice & J Polesel, 'NAPLAN's unintended consequences mean children's learning is suffering', Melbourne Graduate School of Education, University of Melbourne, 2012, <http://education.unimelb.edu.au/news_and_activities/projects/naplan/naplansopinion>, accessed 15 March 2013.

[14] Australian Institute for Teaching and School Leadership, *Australian professional standards for teachers,* AITSL, Melbourne, 2012, <http://www.teacherstandards.aitsl.edu.au>, accessed 15 March 2013.

[15] B Jensen & J Reichl, op. cit.

[16] Australian Education Union, 'Classroom Teacher: Salary/remuneration rates revised September 2018', AEU Federal Office, Melbourne, <http://www.aeufederal.org.au/application/files/3615/3854/3203/CRTSal.pdf, accessed 16 July 2019.

[17] Hobsons Course Finder, 'What you can expect from study in Education and training', Good Universities Guide /Australian Career Information Register, Hobsons, Melbourne, 2013, <http://www.gooduniguide.com.au/ratings/fos/12/ug> and <http://www.gooduniguide.com.au/ratings/fos/12/pg, accessed 15 March 2013.

[18] Australian Curriculum, Assessment and Reporting Authority (ACARA), *National report on schooling in Australia,* ACARA, Sydney, 2019, <https://www.acara.edu.au/docs/default-source/default-document-library/national-report-on-schooling-in-australia-20170de312404c94637ead88ff00003e0139.pdf?sfvrsn=0>, accessed 16 July 2019.

[19] Ministerial Council on Education, Employment, Training and Youth Affairs, *Melbourne declaration on educational goals for young Australians,* MCEETYA, Canberra, December 2008.

[20] P Lambert, 'School of the future', *Professional Educator,* vol. 9, no. 3, September 2010, pp. 6-11.

[21] Adapted from P Ridden & K Belger, 'Starting out', *Classroom,* vol. 14, no. 7, Ashton Scholastic, Lindfield NSW, October 1994, pp. 12-14.

[22] HG Ginott, Teacher and child: A book for parents and teachers, Macmillan, New York, 1972.

[23] U Bronfenbrenner, 'What do families do?' *Institute for American Values,* Winter/Spring, 1991, p. 2, cited in LK Brendtro, 'The vision of Urie Bronfenbrenner: Adults who are crazy about kids', *Reclaiming Children and Youth,* vol. 15, no. 3, 2006, pp. 162-166.

www.ingramcontent.com/pod-product-compliance
Lightning Source LLC
Chambersburg PA
CBHW060320030426
42336CB00011B/1140
* 9 7 8 0 9 9 2 5 4 8 1 3 1 *